SO MANY VOICES

POETIC MATRIX PRESS
AUTHORS' 20TH ANNIVERSARY ANTHOLOGY
1997 TO 2017

EDITED BY
JOHN PETERSON, JAMES DOWNS &
JOE MILOSCH
COVER ART BY MOLLY WELLER

POETIC MATRIX PRESS

POETIC MATRIX PRESS

COVER ART BY MOLLY WELLER
ART FOR RABBIT STORIES BY SCOTT SMITH

copyright © 2017 Poetic Matrix Press. All rights revert to the authors.

ISBN: 978-0-9981469-6-6

All rights reserved. No part of this book may be used or reproduced in any manner whatsoever without written permission, except in the case of quotes for personal use and brief quotations embedded in critical articles or reviews.

Poetic Matrix Press
www.poeticmatrix.com

Acknowledgments

Thanks to all of the authors for the pleasure of working with them over the years. Thanks to James Downs for his friendship and collaboration. Thanks to Joyce Downs for her involvement; Dan Davies, Devon Peterson, Joe Milosch for their contributions over the years. Thanks to Joyce Jenkins and Richard Silberg at Poetry Flash for their ongoing support of poetry and this press over the years including providing many reading opportunities for our poets. Also thanks to our distributor Small Press Distribution (SPD) for years and years of getting poetry out into the world. And to Lightning Source Inc. (LSI) for providing an innovative way for small presses like ours to produce quality books at a reasonable cost.

And most importantly to all of the writers and of course all of the readers who make this small effort of ours exist at all. It has been a pleasure and will continue so for many years.

POETIC MATRIX PRESS

Foreward

Do the articles and comments at the beginning of a volume of poetry seem like they are in the way, keeping you from diving into the poetry you came here to experience? I have felt that way before, but not these days. I find the forewards and introductions add a flavor to volumes like salt and pepper to a stew. They give a context for the book, what it meant to put this collection of art out into the public's hands and some about the magic of the words inside. You the reader are going to have your own experience, your own communication with the words. That is the way it should be. And these preceders only add to your experience.

I have been with Poetic Matrix Press since it's inception. I met John Peterson in 1997 in the high Sierra Mountains at Yosemite National Park. He came from San Diego, by way of the Central Valley. I came from Texas by way of Northern California. We both love poetry. Eventually, we began to meet once a week at his apartment in what had been Mother Curry's residence; later over morning lattes at Degnan's Deli. We talk-shared about everything: poetry, politics, music, Yosemite, sports, Nature, anything. This conclave of two led to John wanting to start putting out a newsletter of discourse and poetry. And so Poetic Matrix Press was born. I was just glad to be involved.

I started writing poetry after high school, through college and into my later work life. Always a hobby, I didn't know it, but I was learning how to write. And I read. Oh, I read. I began to find favorite authors…Robert Frost, Mary Oliver for their involvement in Nature, and Basho, a 17th century Japanese monk/poet who solidified haiku as a form. Writing haiku taught me how to find just the right word as the form only allows for three lines, seventeen beats. Haiku is just like sculpture…you cut away what is not the art until you have what is.

I count my seriousness about poetry to the beginnings of Poetic Matrix Press. I helped Publisher/Editor John Peterson with whatever task I could. I believed in his philosophy, a "humanistic, each person having huge potential, eyes-open to the world" discipline. I still do.

POETIC MATRIX PRESS

And then early on John asked for a volume of poetry from me. I had hand written and produced six small volumes called 'chapbooks' for family and friends. But this would be published professionally! And after working with John as my volume editor, the chapbook came out in 2000, WHERE MANANITA. This blew me away. I never expected to have a publisher. I just walked in on one, of sorts. Often folks want fame from publishing. But my mind went a different direction. I wanted as many folks to have those words in their minds through the volume in their hands. I am still that way.

I have had the fortune to be with the Press when the newsletter turned into chapbooks and then chapbooks into full volumes and now into 20 years of over 40 authors and 50+ full volumes. It certainly has been an exciting, wild ride, helping John keep a small press alive.

And there have been great moments along the way…magical readings with good people reading their works; the excitement when each new volume comes out, and now a 20th anniversary anthology. One of my favorite things to do, as associate editor of the press, is to go out and find new interesting authors to add to our list of folks. And they are such good people, I am glad and proud to know them. I hope you will get a sense of that as you read this volume. Each of these folks have a similar caring for humans and the world view and have expressed their appreciation about being published with this Press's philosophy.

I will conclude this memory exercise with one more thing. Poetic Matrix Press is John Peterson. His spirit, his dedication, his philosophy, his caring and his love are on every page of every volume he has produced. Yes, the press is the authors, but I say the Press is surely John. It would not have happened without him nor continued without him nor reached 20 years. Thank him. Thank him. And I give thanks that he is my best friend. It is through John that you have this wonderful volume in your hands.

James Downs , Associate Editor
Author of MERGE WITH THE RIVER (2004)

Some Additional Notes

Right from the beginning of this press I have been amazed at the diversity of expression. The many voices that truly give rise to the communities that we come from; this is really the reason and the joy in what we do. Poetry really is that thing; it is the authentic voice of a people. And it is quite remarkable that there is such a proliferation of poetry in print today.

I have often told people when discussing this press that it is the joy of working with these authors that is the most important thing for me. I get to engage with poets from so many communities here and across the nation and in other parts of the world. We work together over a period of time to bring out a volume that most perfectly represents what they are trying to say.

We look for and have found many authors from many places that give voice to our goals as a press.

*Poetic Matrix Press is dedicated to publishing quality poetry
by poets that have something to say and the means to say
it well. We look for working poets who have
developed their craft and their imaginal skills.*

The title for this 20th Anniversary Anthology is So Many Voices. Indeed there are so many voices and we need these voices. My motivation for getting into the publication business stemmed from my involvement in the anti-war/civil rights movements. After I returned from Vietnam this country was in turmoil and out of necessity I was drawn into a need to better understand what had happened to me and what had happened to so many others.

I had been writing since I was very young and that continued but at the time it was truly for me to understand myself. That is one of the magical qualities of poetry, it is a means of finding out what is going on inside yourself and your people. Later, with the assistance of Terry

Hertzler, I opened up my own Vietnam experience and I joined with a group of poets to explore our time through poetry.

When I moved with my family to the Central Valley in the early 90s and went to work in Yosemite I realized that I wanted to leave a record of our times. Many of the poets of those early years show up in these pages; Tomás Gayton, Joe Milosch, Brandon Cesmat. Others showed up in the print newsletters we initially sent out and the on-line letters later. As James Downs and I met over many months we clarified what and why we were doing this. We have now in our 20th year put out some 60 titles. We, with so many other voices, will insure that what we have experienced, the pleasures we have known and the understanding we have gained, will touch others in our community and sail off into a future world to, we hope, enliven them and let them know of our world.

Mostly we have published poetry with an occasional non-fiction title, a memoir or two, and a couple of books of philosophical interest.

A few words on just some of our authors. All of our authors will speak in these pages, a few need special note here. First off is Kim Shuck, the newly appointed 2017 Poet Laureate of San Francisco. Kim joins an illustrious list of former San Francisco poet laureates including: Lawrence Ferlinghett, Janice Mirikitanii, devorah major, Jack Hirschman, Diane di Prima, and Alejandro Murguía. Along with the US Poet Laureate, the San Francisco Poet Laureate surely sits in a preeminent place in this country's literary life. Congratulations and great success to her. We had the opportunity to publish her *Rabbit Stories* in 2013. Working with Kim and getting to know her has been a delight. She brought Leroy Moore to our attention as well.

It must also be noted that Kim is not the only Poet Laureate in our midst. Joseph Zaccardi served as Marin County, California Poet Laureate (2013-2015). We had the distinct pleasure of publishing his 2009 volume *Render*. Brought to us by James Downs, Joseph's work is some of the most beautiful and stirring writing on the deepest and most profound understanding of our collective Vietnam era.

With the joys there have been some losses. We had the great joy of getting to know and getting to work with Francisco X Alarcón. Truly he was a man of great glorious passion. Again James introduced him to us. Francisco passed suddenly in January of 2016.

I first met Francisco at a reading in the Library of UC Merced. Immediately I was taken with this man of large intelligence and profound joy and passion. To work with him was a pure pleasure. He knew what he was about and he knew who he was speaking for. It is said that he is one of the great modern Chicano poets and indeed he is and he is a voice for many more; the gay community, the youth, political activists, the earth and its creatures — all of us. The title of his book tells it: *Borderless Butterflies: Earth Haikus and Other Poems / Mariposas sin fronteras: Haiku terrenales y otros poemas*. So many miss him; I miss him.

We also lost another beautiful person a few years earlier; Diana Festa. Our new electronic world allows to get to know many people though too often we miss the chance to have intimate face time with them. I worked with Diana over many months on her book *The Gathering*, 2009. I would like to quote a piece that I wrote for her back cover. "*Curl up by a fire with a glass of port to truly enjoy The Gathering. Ms. Festa opens up very difficult life experiences where she struggles to bring some kind of understanding. We don't see this in poetry all that often and it can make a difficult read to the uninitiated. But the beauty of her language and the depth of her understanding make her subject palatable and carry the reader to that place of truth and beauty to which poetry aspires.*"

Diana was generous and a delight to work with. I am pleased that my dear friend Tomás Gayton did have a chance to spend some time with Diana in one of his sojourns to New York City.

One final vignette here. After completing Yearn Hong Choi's memoir, *Song of Myself: A Korean-American Life* he asked if we would be willing to take on a project with noted Korean poet Mun Duc-su. The project was a translation of Mun's long poem, *The Postman*, with three commentaries. Mun's poem had gained great acclaim in Korea and across the international literary landscape. Ours was a challenging project with

Poetic Matrix Press

Korean characters mixed in the manuscript. Done up in hardcover our modest effort joined the body of Mun Duc-su's work in his presentation as a nominee for the 2010 Nobel Prize in Literature; something he is proud of I 'm sure as are we to have been included.

And now here are *So Many Voices*. It has been my pleasure to be along on this ride and my deepest thanks to James Downs for so much it really cannot be expressed. I do hope he knows.

To all the authors, thank you for allowing us to assist in bringing your voice out into this chaotic world. To the artists that contributed to the cover and interior art, one of our great joys, thank you. To all the editors, graphic designers, photographers, and others who contributed to these works pre and post production, thank you. There are many who have joined in these efforts. To Joyce, Dan, Devon and many others who have been instrumental in advancing this art. The folks at Small Press Distribution, those at Lightning Source Inc., once a list like this is started it can go on and on, thank you all. And to Mary Ellen Wilson who joined us in the beginning and taught us the art of book design, thank you.

> If poets and lovers of poetry don't write, publish,
> read, and purchase poetry books then we will have
> no say in the quality of our contemporary culture
> and no excuse for the abuses of language, ideas,
> truth, beauty, and love in our cultural life.

John Peterson, Publisher 2017

20th Anniversary Authors' Anthology

Contents

Acknowledgments iii
Foreward v
Some Additional Notes vii

So Many Voices

Poetry

Kim Shuck	3	Rabbit and Quantum Theory
	6	Drought Break
Francisco X. Alarcón	7	Haikus terrenales Earth Haikus
	9	Loco Crazy
	10	Federico García Lorca / Roque Dalton / Gloria Anzaldúa
James Downs	11	Geese river
	12	Two Haiku
	13	Someone's burning
	14	Whispers in the grass
	15	Haiku
Raphael Block	16	Other Than Here
	18	Wired
	19	Blue Moon
	20	Once
	21	Frida Kahlo's Self-Portrait with Monkeys
Shadab Zeest Hashmi	22	Window Overlooking the Furn
	23	Montage
	25	I Wished To Write You an Aubad
	26	U.S. Air Strikes
	27	Mosquee de Paris
	28	Guantanamo
	29	War
john (peterson)	30	dark hills
	32	Carin and the Beat Chicks
	34	Ben Webster
	35	wilderness in the city
	36	dark season

— xi

Diana Festa	37	Odors
	38	Selective Recollections
Anne Whitehouse	39	A Blessing and a Curse
	41	Blessing XVI
	43	The Beyond
Joseph Milosch	46	Landscape of a Woman and a Hummingbird
	47	Great Grandfather and the Compost Pile
	48	Why Is a Scar on a Man…
	49	Grandfather
	50	F Is the Shape
	51	A Cricket Is Singing
Patricia Nelson	53	Hero
	54	Sister Eulalia
Brian Bronson	56	The Rebels Cruise
	57	The Lizard King
	58	Camelot Returning
Ashley Gene Pinkerton	59	Only Now
	60	Undone
	61	In Search of You
Dan Tharp	62	Oscar
	63	Morning Colors
Joe O'Connell	64	Music-energy
	65	Fair Day
	69	Halloevening
Joan Michelson	70	Lament
	71	Song For Sleep
	72	Bosnian Girl
Leroy Franklin Moore, Jr.	73	Little Boy of the Blues
	76	Moan To Me
	78	Brown Krips Holding & Becoming Internationally
J. P. Linstroth	80	Wallowed
	81	Picasso's Fragments
Lyn Lifsin	83	It's Dark, it's Shirt-Soaking Hot
	84	130 to 150 Bodies a Day
	85	On the Day Rushing to the Metro Already a Little Late…
	86	Malala Dreams of Military Helicopters

Rayn Roberts	87	The Last Garden in Aleppo
	88	In Aleppo, a Haven of Beauty
	89	Of One and Many Worlds
	90	Each Morning Begins a Journey Until You Arrive At Who You Are
	92	Lament for the Body Politic
	93	Reminiscence
Joel Netsky	94	As the Explorer
	95	At Glance
Chris Hoffman	96	Handies Peak
	97	Oasis
	98	Advice from the Last Loon
J. C. Olander	100	Comets
	102	Blue Earth
Molly Weller	103	On Finding Myself on the Map
	104	Quilter's Burden
	105	Jornada del Muerto
	106	Apple Orchard
Charles Entrekin	107	Hay Stacker
	109	Day After the Market Crash
Charles & Gail Rudd Entrekin	110	Forgiveness
	111	Nature Noir
	112	Chronic Lymphocytic Leukemia
	113	Before Making Love
Gail Rudd Entrekin	114	Blue Whales
	115	Snoring
	117	Rearrangement of the Invisible
	118	Something Coming
	119	Blue Moon
	120	Nepenthe
Sandra Lee Stillwell	121	Seeing Coyote
	123	In A Dress Made Of Butterflies
	125	For Mouska
Tomás Gayton	127	Winds of Change (English)
	128	Vientos de Cambio (Spanish)
	129	Bahia (English)
	130	Bahia (Spanish)
	131	Mexico's Forgotten Negros (excerpt)

Brandon Cesmat	133	Why Do Black Lives Matter?
	134	Driven Into the Shade
	137	The Long Pass
	139	Light in All Directions
	140	Pine Speak
	141	Howl, Hoot and Poem Disguised
	142	Queen Calafia at Home
Adam Funk	144	Apeirophobia
	145	Life
	146	Scene Rhapsodic
Richard Kovac	148	To The Reader / A Modest Disclaimer
	149	The Banner of the Last Hippie
	150	Taken for Granted
	151	Obit for the Twin Towers
	152	Laboring Forth
	153	Keats' Hoax
Lee Underwood	154	I don't know much about God,
	155	For Tim Buckley
Arthur W. Campbell	157	Introduction
	158	Further Freedom-Law Adventures
Mun Duk-su	161	from the Forward by Yearn Hong Choi
	161	from The Postman
Joseph Zaccardi	165	There is a River
	166	Walking in the Woods Toward Jade Mountain
	167	Black Sand River
	168	Celestial Stems, Earthly Branches
Grace Marie Grafton	169	Evoke
	170	Revelation

NON-FICTION

Hassan El-Tayyab	172	from Chapter 26
Ruth Rosenthal	175	In the Midst of Plenty
	177	In the Garden of Life
Yearn Hong Choi	178	Introduction
	179	A Korean-American Life in Washington / Literary Activities
	180	Yearn Hong Choi poem
	180	Second Poetry Reading ...
	181	Black Korean

Steven Soo Hyun Kim

Bonnie Joanna Gisel ed.
Peter and Donna Thomas
Reverend James Fox
Alex Landon &
    Elaine Halleck
Daniel D. Davis
Shelton Kenneth Peterson

Peter Gibson Friesen

LISTING OF ALL
POETIC MATRIX PRESS TITLES
AND IMPRINTS (PM BOOKS,
PM LIBRARY, KVASIR BOOKS)
BY PUBLISHING DATE;
WITH AUTHOR BIOGRAPHY

182 Reminiscence
183 Introduction (excerpts)
185 Hunger, Despair, and Funeral (excerpt)
187 Quotes by John Muir
188 Introduction
191 Happiness Is Thinking For One's Self
193 Introduction

195 Foreward (excerpts)
198 Foreward
200 December 7, 1941
201 August 15, 1945
203 from the Preface

205

SO MANY VOICES

—Poetry—

POETIC MATRIX PRESS

Rabbit Stories
by Kim Shuck

Rabbit and Quantum Theory

If you put a quantum scientist in a box and never open it again will anyone ever understand the uncertainty principle? What does the uncertainty principle have in common with Native American philosophy? If I do not set foot on the scale between mid-November and mid-January did my weight actually spike in December? Why does anything care if I measure it?

I see Rabbit. He is weighing and measuring leaves so that they can exist, so that he can effect their existence with his regard. We are all in community, the subatomic particles wait for Rabbit's gaze so that they can dance in the music he makes by looking. He takes this responsibility very seriously, making sure to look at them during auspicious and ceremonial times. Rabbit is careful with the subatomic particles. The ground does not have the ability, after all, to support his weight unless he takes the next step. He is careful not to think about the Ukten while he is looking at the particles. Instead he whispers, "beautiful, happy" he cradles them in his sight and they dance.

It is difficult to find either the scientist willing to be boxed for the sake of theory or the box that would contain her. She is busy after all, measuring her own corner of the cosmos. Not, I hasten to reassure you, putting mustard seeds into stolen skulls. She is watching the dance... well, that and doing laundry. Even quantum scientists can't avoid the laundry. That experiment insists upon being measured. It is like the old-time water clocks: time will stop if there is no laundry to drip from drawer to bin, a brief moment on the skin in-between. She knows that she has a variety of measuring tools available. Pleasure in the feel of clean cotton on skin, although difficult to get funded, is certainly one of her tools.

Rabbit spends his weekend being a rabbit. He munches contraband cilantro, intended for the family quesadillas and contemplates overlaps between theoretical physics and Green Corn ceremony. It is important to take responsibilities seriously, he munches in a rabbity way. Later he will sprawl floppily, he has chosen to be a lop this weekend, enjoys the softness of this form, its acuity of taste. Things like to be thanked so he plans an experiment of thanks, decides to conduct it in the spring rather than the fall. There is enough silliness about thankfulness in the fall already, thinks Rabbit.

At the pow wow people dance. Circle the arena. As men and women look at each other in all combinations, they dance to the music of the looking, to the music of being looked at. This weekend no one drops any feathers.

Rabbit makes sure to measure himself in the mirror every day. Quantum self-definition, he thinks. Pinching an inch of extra waistline, he smiles to himself, evidence of good stew past. He exposes his teeth, sucks thoughtfully, considering things to chew. Soon he will go back to the pow wow to look and look and look and whisper things to the people as he looks, "beautiful, happy". He cradles them all in his sight and they dance dance dance dance.

The quantum physicist, her grandma and a collection of Aunties sit at the kitchen table. A large rabbit has claimed space under the table, where the physicist used to sit with her crayons and her magnets and her collection of small empty bottles. A suspicious smell of cilantro wafts up towards her. She listens to the Aunties as they talk of stew, the making of stew, the dishing up of stew and the relative merits of various root vegetables. The physicist ponders all possible meanings of the word 'relative'. A munching sound from below provides counterpoint. She has been promoted to the space above the table… wonders if this means she is becoming an Auntie. Maybe Rabbit has the right idea, remaining below.

There is a wild rose that the people call Rabbit Food. Rabbit licks his lips at the thought. Beauty thy name is Rabbit Food. He imagines a vine trailing up a paw paw. The tree is heavy with fruit. He has thought about every leaf, every blossom and naturally every bit of fruit. Rabbit sighs and looks at the legs of beautiful women, of women who discuss food. He knows their names, these women… and one is named for that rose. Rabbit Food is talking about stew, about potatoes, about spicebush… and especially about bean bread. She is more beautiful than he remembers her, even though he thinks of each of her cells singing happily every day. He thinks about the beautiful lines he is singing around her eyes, they are not finished yet, but they are a song of smiling.

She has been plagued by Rabbit all of her life. How could she not have been? What had they been thinking with that name? Now there was no cilantro in the fridge… and she thinks that a certain tubby lop might well be to blame. Ah well. It is time to gather the clothes in from the line. She feels that small closed boxes are suspect, even those that dry the laundry. Besides, there is such riot of plant life to cradle the wash in happy thoughts. She doesn't know all of them, but they smell like happy thoughts. Such song and dance for the creek underground at the foot of the garden, this is so good for the sub-atomic particles in the laundry. No telling what the effect might be on that experiment. The experiment would have to run its course.

There is a certain wildness to this garden. Rabbit finds a damp and shady spot and greedily eyes the berries to be. He makes promises of undying love to the berry canes. Truly, what could be more undying than being together forever… and he intends to eat them up, to add their songs to his, to become the box and the contained, and to sing them in his cells for all time.

She spreads sheets crisp with the songs of plum tree, of apple blossom, of milkweed and of Rabbit. With so many military folk in the family she knows the right way to tuck in sheets. You can bounce a quarter off of a bed that she makes, no mistake.

Rabbit becomes both softer and more clever in this garden. He watches the striped spider weave. She rarely has time for him, he learned long ago not to disturb her weavings. He blinks warily at the memory. Spider, serious as she is, enjoys Rabbit's company, but the only clue is her slightly more formal posture. She weaves intently. Measuring everything carefully she creates her web, her blanket.

The physicist had saved the quilt for last. The sheets are for the military men in the family; the quilts… well the quilts she'd learned about from the Grandmothers. She spreads this quilt gently. It is soft from love and use, soft from thoughts and experiments. Each piece of the quilt is its own thing. The quantum physicist settles her inheritance onto the bed and goes off to stir stew.

New poem by Kim Shuck
2017 Poet Laureate of San Francisco

Drought Break

Weaving of water is layered
Sitting in the rain
Feet dragging in the runoff
I know there are trees coming down tonight
Drought tired
Clots of soil run free
Sailors still catch and spill
Windpainting
Still navigate by song
Remember
Remember
Treesong
Waterweave
So far we are still witness

BORDERLESS BUTTERFLIES: EARTH HAIKUS AND OTHER POEMS
MARIPOSAS SIN FRONTERAS: HAIKUS TERRENALES Y OTROS POEMAS
by Francisco X. Alarcón

Haikus terrenales

poema primordial —
el latido maternal
de nueve meses

21 de marzo de 2011

la noche — taza
de café vertida sobre
el mantel terrenal

4 de julio de 2011

súbitamente
los paisajes son poemas
y el camino es página

4 de enero de 2012

si un árbol cae
¿quién lo lee? — el mejor
libro aún es árbol

7 de febrero de 2012

todos somos hojas
temblando, cayendo
de un baobab de África

17 de marzo de 2012

Earth Haikus

primordial poem —
the maternal heartbeat
of nine months

March 21, 2011

the night — a cup
of black coffee poured over
the Earth's tablecloth

July 4, 2011

all of a sudden
landscapes become poems
and the road is a page

January 4, 2012

if a tree should fall
who will read it? — the greatest
book is yet a tree

February 7, 2012

we all are leaves
trembling, falling from
an African baobab

March 17, 2012

flores / cantos
canto flores —
floricantos

girasol
Sol Flor
floricanto Sol

Sol / Luna / luz
Luz lunar
Luz solar

por amor a la Luna
luciérnagas dan luz
en la oscuridad

todos somos uno —
¿somos todos uno?
uno todos somos

26 de marzo de 2012

flowers / songs
song flowers —
flowersongs

sunflower
Flower Sun
Sun flowersong

Sun / Moon / light
Moonlight
Sunlight

twinkling fireflies
in love with the Moon
swirl in the night sky

we all are one —
are we all one?
                one we all are

March 26, 2012

Loco

mis puertas
las dejo
sin cerrar

los extraños
me parecen
tan familiares

a todos
los abrazaría
y besaría

cada día
en la calle
hallo a Dios

en vez
de llorar
ahora me río

quiero poner
el mundo
al revés

nada
me convence —
debo de estar loco

3 de agosto de 2009

Crazy

I leave
my doors
unlocked

strangers
look to me
so familiar

I would
embrace and
kiss them all

every day
on the street
I run into God

instead
                of crying
now I laugh

I want to
turn the world
upside down

nothing
sways me —
I must be crazy

August 3, 2009

Federico García Lorca / Roque Dalton / Gloria Anzaldúa

oh poetas del mundo	o poets of the world
de ayer, mañana, siempre	from yesterday, tomorrow
sin fronteras	forever borderless
hermano del alma	soulmate brother
hermano en lucha	brother in struggle
hermana mestiza	Mestiza sister
pusieron en riesgo	you risked your lives
sus vidas en versos — y ante	in poems — choosing
mentiras, la verdad	truth over lies
9 de diciembre de 2013	December 9, 2013

Merge with the River
James Downs

Geese   river

I look up   surprised
to see three geese   bountiful
black long curving necks   ending in

white bonnets and black beaks   rocking
back and forth as they mutely
swim up river

they turn and stop at a bank
to turn bugs   this trio
of hungry angels

one on the bank lifts
her neck on high
looking   white-bottomed birds of grace:

the irony of it   you want to see
geese in flight   but then they would be
gone   swimming one at a time in a line

wings folded back along sleek and sassy bodies
you sense they know of things
you will never see in your time   but

oh to witness world-curving necks   they fly
in a ballet of white and black
and call out to each other "geese" "river"

Two Haiku

Thousand leaves in breeze
    buddhist bells ringing   silence
that follows   deafens

I enter naked
   midnight moon   nooday sun   and
sense always   deep light

Someone's burning

Sit at round blank small table
on second floor heaven
poetry room of city lights books

look out the window at pigeons and
someone's laundry   hung out
to dry   nervous eyes   the pigeons

look about and rise to the bleating
of fire sirens   someone's burning
house   it's a ritual thing

piegeons   don't see me   their backs to
building   blazed by sun   but i
snuck our books of poetry

onto the shelves   among so many
other magicians   alchemy spins
something's gone to gold   and fire

New poems James Downs

Whispers in the grass

The sheer
abruptness of sweetness
on the tongue

the full
dawning of sunflowers
in the mind

the repetitive
mirror taken down
off the wall

the shouldered
certainty of sighings
in the throat

what is it we seek in this life of woe

the twinkled
brightness of benevolence
near the stars

the tried-
and-true of whispers
in the grass

the hunger danger of hope in the heart

Haiku

green rounded trees 'round
    green springs road gauge sacred way
to another space

Spangling Darkness
poems and songs by Raphael Block

Other Than Here

Most of my life
I'm drawn to places
other than here.

Of course, in hungry youth
I needed to travel
there.

Throughout adulthood
my thoughts and desires propel
into the stratospheres
or am I led
by an invisible noose?

Affects fling me into
fierce mountain passes
battling tribes
precipitous chasms.

Memories magnetically
sway me towards fading
frayed flowers.

Occasionally I visit here
when stunned by
a sudden scent, sound
or a look—

when my emotions sputter
into tears and between
the cracks of defeat
and relief
fresh vistas appear—

when feelings zing
at the amazing beings
planted about an
unblinkered view.

But how long
can I bear
to touch here
smell here
re-find here
before drifting off anew?

Wired

First She had to heave up mountains,
then cool her blood with ice and wait
a little while for rock to tumble
shatter, allow her glacier plow
to rake the valleys out, until
the last few seconds, so they say,
we came and settled, built dry walls
up to the crags, scattered sheep to eat
forest shoots, and so came pasture.

And still her brooks course through
her veins, lilting and sighing and
spinning their ways into lake and sea
as she tilts quietly
ominous, egg-timer wired
to our words, feelings, thoughts—
weighing whether to flip it over
or, like the show with too small
an audience, simply close the stage.

Strings of Shining Silence   Earth-Love Poems
by Raphael Block

Blue Moon

The moon came to sip
    dew at my table, and liking it,
        stayed awhile.

Soon she slipped into a nearby
    puddle to dip and bathe,
        bending the trees
           with her glory.

The cat, desperate
    to join this lunar party,
        caterwauled like crazy
           until I padded up
                to grant his wish.

He sprinted toward
    her silvery sheen,
        only to find
           she had whisked
                back into the sky

leaving us both behind
    yowling and baying.

Once

After John Donne (1572-1631)

Once, your arched feet and limbs stretched
to tease the ground, your gesturing
arms sang to the sky, the swish of your black skirt
overturned my heart. But now, they've wound
themselves into a stranglehold around
this tightened chest. Expel my breath!
Plow these barren furrows! Seven Sisters light
all my belly's sorrows. When will Orion
sheathe his sharp sword that stabs so darkly
in the night? Will the ocean waves bear my despair
on their ceaseless slap and roll?
Ah! But this salted grief
has sweetened — the tears I pour
taste more and more like seasoned wine.

Frida Kahlo's *Self-Portrait with Monkeys*

Their dark eyes are filled with questioning innocence. Hers are weary and aching. Their small hands grip her blouse, an arm clasps her neck, as if they, too, understand the weight of great sadness. Half-hidden by lily leaves, they squat and stand with momentary restraint.

Her body knows that the bird of paradise will wilt, die, and come again—that her white-breasted monkey friends will burst into cacophonous chatter, and vanish through the shaking, screeching tree-tops as suddenly as they appeared. This fragrant flame is her one hope.

So she carefully braids and ties her thick, black hair above her ashen face, propels herself to the easel, toward the blank canvas that has waited through the long, tremulous night for a blood infusion from her molten depths.

Baker of Tarifa
Poems by Shadab Zeest Hashmi

Window Overlooking the *Furn*

The dough lies dreaming
Pregnant
and smooth in an earthen basin
It is summer and the soap white curtains
are exhaling like sails

There is far away laughter
And a pulse nearby
in oil
semolina

She catches the pulse
the imprint of fate-lines

It is the summer
Of barley white flour spiced honey lavender sourdough
From the houses of Jewish leather merchants
Christian boatmen singers
Muslim botanists

Held by a mother
with kohl-lined eyes

Bread
for apricot-skinned children

Montage

The Andalusian
is known for sensitivity and intelligence.

A Christian Chronicler writes of Muslims:
"The handsomest among them
was as black as the cooking pot."

Adafina is a cooking pot
used by Jews. It is buried
in embers on Friday night.
The meal is ready
the next day.

On Friday
Muslims are advised
to take the long way home
after prayer
so they can greet neighbors.

Christians
must love their neighbor
as themselves.

Adafina
comes from "dufn" or "buried" in Arabic.

The Andalusian is often
drawn with black pigment.

Arabic is a Semitic language.

Burnt bones were
used to make black.

The Andalusian is mostly gray
and rarely has a pearl,
buckskin or chestnut
coat.

The highest commandment
For Jews, Muslims and Christians:
Love God with all your heart, soul
And mind.

The Andalusian is prized
as a war horse .

Kohl and Chalk
by Shadab Zeest Hashmi

I Wished To Write You an Aubad

Instead of walking the night in Paris,
letting our eyes be the sharply defined pansies
the nasal city has so longed for,
we shut ourselves in a room
that was no friend,
and carved one argument after another.
Instead of gazing
at the Mona Lisa in the Louvre,
we bought a black and white print
(of a man climbing a coconut palm)
from a youth who claimed
that the money will go to a scholarship fund.
We hoped never to be friendless or in need.

What was there about the place
but loftiness? A mistaken sense of perfume.
Less distinct than lulling. So we went
to the marketplace which smelled of cheese.
Flat, cold fish. And swollen bread.

I wished to write you an aubade.
Instead, I gazed at the early morning river
lit by Impressionistic dots of light
through the life-size glass
of the train door,
and your reflection superimposed on it.

U.S. Air Strikes

In the four minutes
it took me to mince the cloves,
dump the tea leaves
in the rose bush,
and soap the carafe,
a whole city was lost.

There were feet still in school shoes,
limp flesh singing into satchels,
clinging to a post, a shattered clock.
The children, if not orphaned
were purpled beyond recognition.

Orders had been carried down,
one signal igniting another.
And a man had let a deafening rhapsody
guide his young hand to drop
a five hundred pound bomb
on a mosque.

Just when I finished rinsing the carafe,
a whole city was under cement dust and smoke,
and I thought I heard screaming behind walls of fire
in the kettle's sharp whistle,
just when I added the cloves,
the last green lime.

Mosquee de Paris

Ablution water,
opal
on a worshipper's
slipper left by the doorstep:
She will travel far
and return before its sparkle has dropped.

Gold and ink on parchment
dyed blue
speaks of duty to the widow and the wayfarer.

Light caught on pink marble
swirls into an open ear.

Eggs in the outstretched hands
of an old woman in Kabul
For the widows of New York
The American author takes them trembling
Insha'Allah.

If there were no kindness
conversation would be useless,
Rumi says. His guides:
A goldsmith, a desert wanderer, a scribe.

Stitched to silence,
you and I wander the same places,
wearing zipped shoes.

Guantanamo

A guard forces you to urinate on yourself
Another barks out louder than his dog
the names of your sisters
who live in the delicate nest
of a ruby-throated hummingbird
Each will be a skeleton he says
Was there someone who gave you
seven almonds for memory,
a teaspoon of honey every morning?
Cardamom tea before bed?
Someone who starched your shirts
in rice water, then ironed them?
Held your chin
To say the send-off prayer
before school?
You're tied to a metal coil
And memory
is a burnt wire.

War

Tremolo of teacups
Scissoring sirens

Two streets ripped apart

Flesh-eating clocks
Clock-eating wheels

A time of boots
A town of tires

The night has accrued sap
to trap us
in its amber

Dark Hills and Wild Mountains
by john (peterson)

dark hills

the hills are dark even in the hot
startling sun they seem dark
oak trees that in the night are silhouettes
are little more in the day time
blue oak and live oak roots wound to granite
dark branches firm black trunks
are a portend of the invisible roots
in the night unintentional probing lights
momentarily bring them into view
then easily they settle
to a more natural place
in the closer darkness
she sat on the pounding engine compartment
its burnt wood color disappearing
buttons loosened
landscape of wrestling coyotes
in the waning moon light
gives them form a hint
a calming surge
they demand little yet they are deceiving
and you are inundated
caught in magic and you cannot get out
constantly enraptured dreadnought intrigue
in the late afternoon after unseasonal rains
hills are distracting
colors in heavy contrast blending together
in the next moment

at night tree lines are slate black
run together
filled with tints and hues
alabaster lights but you must involve
you must seek
then you are never loosened

a thousand hills roll the same electric swelling
then slow
to a thickening of movement
they yield yet never release
in the dark on sloping curves
a mystery takes form in the valley below
clothes are on the floor
motor with the road
fire with the slow moving of the hills
with the moon
playing across ragged granite outcroppings
watching the road
watching her orange shape
burnt orange mixed with grazing fields
with the same light that catches
the voluntary edge of the sorcerers
dwelling placewatching the road

watching her eyes dark
at the edge of the world
her legs in shadow
the road turns once twice
around shaping curvatures
into shadow her shoulders inside
the low hum inside the longing call
lights recede
further the road ceases the moon descends
behind an etched illusion
treeline dissolves insider her glance
her hair the smell of manzanita deer brush
the hills are gone
the lights
are great distances

Poetic Matrix Press

News of the Day   Poems of the Times
by John (Peterson)

Carin and the Beat Chicks
Beat Conference - 1994

Listening to "Beat Chicks",
Hattie, Joyce, Carolyn, Jan,
I thought of you.

I don't know where you are now
but you did the road way back.

You didn't hit the road with the guys
you did it yourself, catchin' rides from
California to Iowa—

I remember a photograph of you
sittin' on the porch of an old Iowa farm.

What our older sisters couldn't do,
you and your sisters did years later.

Your road is still way out there.

Some day you'll tell your younger
sisters how it was in the 70s,
hitch hikin' on the road
in the *u s of a* without fear.

No fear that your brothers on the road
would harm you.

Tell your sisters
that it was this way once,

When the innocent
were free
and we did love each other.

Ben Webster

Letting go of shady images, smoky
bars and rain soaked streets,
Mike Hammer lost in the night.

Tall downtown buildings—
street light shadow image,
smoky place on ribs and long sighs—
piano string before the felt hammer hits.

I remember a night long ago,
sitting in the dark looking out the bay window,
sound of a moving baseline—
neighborhood reachin' in.

Old gray man—
piano riff rising easy off of blue pavement.

I'd never seen this middle class suburb
like it had a rhythm
'til I got inside the breath sound
soft and cool,
Ben Webster sax
beatin' out a dark place,
no matter where it sits—

Behind us
all.

The Nature of Mountains
poems by john (peterson)

wilderness in the city

the place where possum and skunk walk
where hawk circles and cries out

where winter clouds overcome
the reputation of beach and sun

a small spread of blue
the slightest touch of a breeze

everything else asphalt and steel
rough side of buildings and planted trees

nothing made before the first necklace
of fertile beads chipped from black rock

and flung out at the wild creature that
would join the wild creature within

making a looping circle recognition of cycles
the goddess without voice
here before all this asphalt and steel

dark season

we keep finding small places that let the
smell of herbs come through

rosemary before its put in the black skillet
with potatoes onions and black pepper

basil oregano and cilantro growing on the roof
top deck where the sound of pigeons and sunsets
fill the sky and early morning bells
from the methodist steeple
stand out against the snow covered peaks
of the cuyamacas

the source of rain in the spider plant
the deep smell of burning oak
eucalyptus both wet and shining and played out in smoke

this is the season the bear sleeps where you and i
slowly give in and lay front to back like spoons in
a velvet embrace

The Gathering
poems by Diana Festa

Odors
After Umberto Eco's
The Mysterious Flame of Queen Loana

The soil's peculiar smell,
fog filtering into clusters of trees,
rain on pavement,
the earthy odor of artichokes,
sweetness of sage, salt in sea air,
pungent tea leaves steaming
in blades of sun—
the planet is saturated with scents.
But there is the desperate loneliness
of parallel lines, unscented, untouching
in a firmament of curves and corners,
seeking solace, a whiff of life
in fragrances.
I navigate among them
in sun-drenched breeze from the desert,
mountains that repeat mountains.
Every step holds
traces of forgotten aims—
and oh, the fear of not finding
the way home.
I do not know how to land
on solid ground, or change my course,
how to leave my parallel-line solitude,
the weighty suspense
in the allegory of loss.

Selective Recollections

> *Happy families are all alike.*
> Tolstoy: Anna Karenina

Little gifts, a Limoges saucer, a Murano flower—
a cumulous of objects in cumulous of years.
I forget who gave the saucer, a vase, a pitcher.
There were letters, often so lovely
they may still be warming pages in some books.
But most went, buried
with days of the past, love notes, dried flowers.
When I left the old house, I walked away
from a cabinet where faces stilled
by the camera smiled in distant sun—
the children, the man I loved.
I hold a convergence of lights in my memory,
and there is no room for photographs
with their unchanging mien.
Remembrance makes its own choice,
elective instants within recurring images.
What do I remember of you?
A myriad instants—
walks at the beach in paling dusk, dinners
at our favorite restaurant, afternoons
by book stalls along the Seine, rocking train rides—
nothing extraordinary,
the simple story we shared,
the quiet pace of our days,
the rhythm of our breathing.

BLESSINGS AND CURSES
poems by Anne Whitehouse

A Blessing and a Curse

One summer afternoon in the 1980s
when the air was fetid and muggy
and the city streets filthy and miserable,

I impulsively looked for refuge
in the American Museum of Natural History,
that storehouse of human knowledge

of what lies within our universe and ourselves,
with its millions of artifacts and specimens,
the accumulations of generations

of explorers among isolated peoples
and unpeopled regions, of the unrecorded past
collected, investigated, and placed into context.

**

I don't remember how I ended up in the room
where the Buddhist monks were making a Mandala
by pouring colored sands from little bottles

to form intricate patterns. They worked their designs
on a tray on a table in the middle of the room,
while viewers watched and cameras recorded their moves.

Three men with shaved heads in saffron robes:
one was older, and two were young. As soon
as I entered, I felt their peace and wanted to stay.

One of the younger monks explained
how the museum had invited them to New York
from their monastic exile in northern India.

They carried the images they made in their heads.
The Mandala would take two months to finish.
"And then?" I asked. He smiled, and his gold tooth

winked at me. "We will take the Mandala
to the Hudson River and offer it to the water.
The museum wants to preserve it.

They will use sprays to fix the sands,
but they won't work. It will be given back;
the cycle must continue."

I remember the lightness in his voice,
the rippling muscles of his lifted arms,
a grace that seemed without sex, outside of time.

I was older than he, though still apprentice
to my art.   I thought of the beautiful designs

of the Wheel of Life, their inner meanings
and mysteries, and the interplay of colors.

It seemed tragic to me, but not to him.
His inner equilibrium wasn't disturbed.

It mattered not to him that nothing lasted,
and I counted it a blessing and a curse.

Blessing XVI

There is something to be said
for being a renter,
of watching over a place
without the obligation
to improve it.

The Native Americans
made it a practice
to leave little trace of themselves
on the landscape.

Few of us can bear
to travel so lightly.
Yet this is our condition:
to occupy this life,
knowing we will
be parted from it,
but not when.

At sunset my shadow stretches
over the sea as I ease myself in
for the last swim of summer.
For thirty years I've immersed
in the cold waters of this cove
and felt cradled by sea and sky.
In their ever-changing immensities
I sense the unpossessable sublime.

I sink my restless thoughts to silence
so I may cleave to my true purpose.

Tethered, words enter the mind
through the eye or the ear,
to make of themselves
the weightless structure
apprehended wholly or in part,
like a shape shifting in the mist,
reverberant as a song,
to be taken up or forgotten,
like spent desire, or sunlight
shining on water, a fading reflection.

New poem by Anne Whitehouse

The Beyond
In memory of Margaret Goddard Holt

I

Like frozen soapsuds on a sea
of pavement, the blanket of snow
is now diminished. All that's left
is the shape of a nerve spreading
over the sidewalk. Twinkling
with crystals, specked with black dirt,
it's proof of the co-existence
of beauty and ugliness.

Two winters' passings prolong
the separation, but still she is scorched
by the memory of that fire
which fed on the peace of the world,
consuming, among thousands,
her husband's life, leaving
a charred ruin the shape of fear
now dismantled, but not in mind.

As solace against the horror
of her thoughts of his last thoughts,
she pictures, as if visible
in the space beyond the space
of the lost towers, a net
of cybermessages that went un-
answered, as if each word
of love were a light or sound

creating together a shimmer
of music, an illuminated web
that endures, inapprehensible
to us, but not to *them* — Spirits!
She longs to know what *they* know:
Are *they* simply in touch with the truth?
The way things *really* are, uncluttered
by personal encumbrances?

In those days as she searched
and searched and he wouldn't
be found, she asked repeatedly
where was he — beyond the dust
in the atmosphere that lingered
for months. Am I already a spirit,
too, for good or ill? she wondered,
unable to mark that transformation,
bridging the separation.
What she'd like most is to partake
of this life-after-death experience
while still alive, so she would *know*.
But life's condition is ignorance.
She thinks how she might think *his* thought.
Those actual inklings of *him*. In *her*.
This is also her link, her claim to faith.

II

The beating of wings resounds
under the steeply pitched roof
of the New York Buddhist Church.

Pigeons roost under the rustic eaves,
and bird lime stains the conical hat
of the great bronze statue of
Shinran Shonin, gazing serenely
over Riverside Drive and the Hudson.

So he must have looked in the ruins
of Hiroshima, and ever before
and after, brought to New York
to symbolize lasting hope
for world peace: the merchant city
where that bomb was first conceived
has less reason and more need
of hope now, after the towers' fall.

She sought out his tranquility
when her eyes confronted too much dust —
graves in the air, a smudge in the sky,
and the dust grown finer and finer,
washed into the earth and sea,
or suspended in our atmosphere.
After the explosion died away,
she heard bells pealing faintly,
as if they had always been there,
but were only rarely heard,
when the other noises ceased.

Landscape of a Woman and a Hummingbird
by Joseph Milosch

Landscape of a Woman and a Hummingbird

He twists his neck to catch the sun,
which turns his throat to the same shade
of red as the fluid in the gourd-shaped feeder.

Peeling grilled tomatoes, she lifts her head
to see him dip his beak, turn his head,
and burst into shadow.

As they slip through her fingers, tomato seeds
become prayer beads, which seem suspended
for a moment before falling into her salsa.

Great Grandfather and the Compost Pile

Light clouds appeared along the upper edge
of that photo of winter wheat and snow.
Shadows hid below shadows as he worked
the compost with a pitchfork.

Standing out of range of the lens, I became
mesmerized by his unhurried strokes.
Lifting his fork, he turned it so that
the mulch fell like feed from a scoop.

Frozen in mid flap, his shirt-tail exposed his rump
where crickets, moths, and ants were attached
by a web. After taking the picture, grandma laughed
and promised to show it during the holidays.

In those days he sat at the head of the table and chewed
the end of his cigar. I sat on his lap as he mumbled
what could have been lyrics to a peasant song, and
unintelligible as they were, I knew them as the words

a man passes to his offspring. He wanted me to know
how to hand-milk cows, or how to mend harnesses,
or shoe a horse. This was his gift, as unknowable
as the pastures and barns of his homeland.

Above the pile his pitchfork swept through egg shells
and corn husks. As I watched him, we shared our breath
with the incoming blizzard.

The Lost Pilgrimage Poems
by Joseph Milosch

Why Is a Scar on a Man...

Why is a scar on a man a mark of distinction,
on a woman a mark of disfigurement?

       I don't know.

Why is it funny when a man loses his hair,
and tragic when a woman loses hers?

       I don't know.

Could you make love to a bald headed woman?

What will you tell her
when the X-Rays turn the scar
on her breast raw-
hamburger red?

When she's bald, lost her eyebrows,
and lies closed-eyed
with a skeletal look,
will you kiss her
and tell her
she's beautiful?

       I don't know.

What do you do
in the bedroom,
when she is thinking
of death
and she cries?

       I hold her hand and I breathe.

Grandfather
1900-1992

He talked as if endearing himself to me
was not the reason he taught me to drive,
or taught me how to set a spark plug gap.
I remember the hose under the kitchen porch.
Grandfather's thumb pulled down his bottom lip,
as he rinsed out old chew, and washed his hands.

I drove him past a stump, a burned down barn,
a rusting pump, a gate where black birds perched.
His quick eyes caught pheasants above the corn,
the train's shadow on stalks. He knew the time
required to drive across the tracks and asked,
"Can you beat it?" Then bared his gold-rimmed tooth.

If we could take a ride through Michigan,
his thumbs thumping the steering wheel, he'd talk
about the bridge at Mackinaw, and I
wouldn't dream of light beneath a brass-edged door,
a cricket singing in his fist, and wake
to raise the blind and see a hawk in flight.

POETIC MATRIX PRESS

New poems by Joesph Milosch

F Is the Shape

During the winter, the wood stove only heated the kitchen in this
two-story house, which is why F was the shape two boys made as they slept
in the same bed. During the Depression, the oldest boy, Bob,
slept with the two younger boys.

In those years, the three brothers formed an E in the bed. When the war
began, the oldest boy left for the Pacific. Out of respect, the two kept
his place in the bed. On Christmas Eve, Bob stood in the door,
listening to his brothers breathe in their sleep.

It was at half past midnight. He was on leave to recover from
second-degree burns on his arms. The sleeves of his uniform hid his
bandaged arms. The tape ran from his biceps to his knuckles. With the ship
on fire, a shipmate and he pulled a crew-mate from the flames.

On the count of three, they reached in and pulled the burning sailor
to safety. He blamed the public school system. "If they hadn't taught
me to count to three, I wouldn't have burned myself." That was the story
that he told first in 1943.

After he woke his brother, he learned that the rest of the family
was attending Mid-Night Mass. They went to the kitchen, made coffee,
and waited in the dark. Listening to his stories, they became
silent when the family returned.

When their mother turned on the kitchen lights, she beheld
her oldest son in his uniform. Flanked by his brothers, he smiled at her.
Then, the true meaning of Christmas became visible.

A Cricket Is Singing

During the first spring
after your passing,
I looked out our bedroom
window at the orange tree.
As it blanketed
our bed with the odor
of its blooms,
I recalled the times we
used to lie in this bed
on the weekend
in the afternoon.
I remembered
how you liked the
smell of the tree's
blossoms,
and how you liked
the way the petals
looked as the buds
opened and exposed
their hearts to the bees.
When we were in this
bed last April, the odor
of the orange blossoms
covered us like dew,
and I said,
"Listen,
a cricket
has found his way into
our room.
He sings to his lover,

who cannot find him."
Now,
I am that cricket,
and I sing to my lover,
who has died.
I sing about my arms:
they long to hold her

Spokes of Dream or Bird
Poems by Patricia Nelson

Hero

Is he true, that far thing
with words and hair,
solid shape
that stops hand and eye
and nothing else?

He rides a thistle of light.
He is a thing set off
to alter toward some cliff,
clear star broken by a crooked eye,
a trick of air or distance.

He is a set of edges,
temporary
on our flowering, altering maps.
Disaster turning in a battle,
a song that widens the mouth like a vowel.

Oh let him stay,
or let him falter
somewhere else,
not too close
or too real.

Sister Eulalia

Around me are the heart-high boys
a spill of circles, shadows.
At their level—noise, gust, grab,
pigeons swinging the unguided, windy colors.

What do they know of tall garments,
small grammatical eyes,
blue eyes that move and gather—
that will change them?

You, boy, at the verge of my voice and shadow,
walk your cruel extravagant bag of organs
to the brink, extinct and falling outward. Come here!

I have sailed around
the rocks I see, the hungers I know.
Far behind, the famine, the landlords
A mark on ocean thinner than my upraised child-arm.

I came in a slipping foundering skin.
I brought a will and a God,
a self to pocket like a muttering shell.
I read, I remembered, I extracted.

You, boy, walking glyph for "vessel,"
an object to fill or voyage with an object.
(To sacrifice is to make holy.) See where I will take you!

Always words and intonations to be made useful,
numbers—little black fish to hook and marshal.
And he who owns the table
owns the words.

Poetic Matrix Press

The Bells of Avalon
the shamanic poems of Brian Bronson

The Rebels Cruise

The rebels cruise
out on the edge,
looking for
a hope that's bled,
moving across
the vacant street,
sweating in
the burning heat.

They try to save
their fellow man,
from a most
elusive hand.
See them there,
a rebel band,
make their own
lonely stand.

What is it
in their raucous voice
that leaves us with
our only choice?

Forever

The Lizard King

I am the Lizard King,
I can do anything.
I balanced worlds
on butterfly wings,
give me some wine,
and hear me sing.

I am the Lizard King,
I can do anything.
See me dance
upon a pyre,
and talk about
our love's desire.

I am the Lizard King,
I can do anything.
Let's bring life
to its greatest fruition.
Let's give birth
to the human condition.

Then I sighed,
in a moment died,
and did everything
I could
to be
misunderstood.

I am the Lizard King.
I can do anything.

Camelot Returning

Camelot is close you see,
something like a waking dream,
pressing through the tides of time,
in our minds it comes alive.

Coming down from shores we know,
underneath a gnarled oak,
are the voices from the past
that stir our souls until the last.

We partake in the dinner feasts,
and in the raucous jousting feats.
Then we hear of righteous quests
that takes a toll amongst the best.

Yet it is not enough to merely dream.
This is something that has got to be.
In this time and in this age,
we need a venerable and noble sage.

So put a call throughout the land,
to each and every able woman,
that there is a table waiting
and a dream in need of sating.

Spiraling Forward A Dance through the Cycles of Life
Ashley Gene Pinkerton

Only Now

The world within me
   stood still at the sight of your Love.
How could I have forgotten?
How could I have ever
   let you slip from my mind?
I see you now so clearly,
    so profoundly, you reach out;
      through the ether we are connected
        in the Light of One;
      in the essence of all-that-has
        and ever-will-be.

I have always known you;
   since the time when we combined
      to make the Light of one single star;
        our star, our Soul, wrapped up and
      tied together in eternal Love,
        in infinite and endless Light.

You are everything
   yet you are nothing.
      Or is that me?

Beyond separation,
   I can feel the edges fading away,
and I can grasp no longer
   that which once was, for it is only now,
      in this moment, that we have ever been.

Undone

Do you think the flower fears its death
as it stretches towards the Light?
Extending forth, unraveling petals,
guided by a silent call,
it surrenders, to embrace what is meant to be.

In Search of You

It was essential that I climb through
>	the depths of my suffering, encompassed in the darkness.

It was there that I found the strength and courage
>	to claw my way back to the surface of awareness.

It was then that I realized I must remember
>	how I had gotten to this place.

I would journey through this darkness again,
>	but not in search of my own heart,
>>		in search of yours.

A Rose in the Briar Patch
poems by Dan Tharp

Oscar

We dropped his ashes from the bridge
into the Canadian River below;
left our words upon the breeze and

watched the current
        sweep him away...
followed soon by two carp

        and an empty can of beer.

Morning Colors

Morning colors
play upon the clouds –
in oranges, reds
and pretty pastels –

And were I to feel
the morning breeze
play about
as it would please;
brush up against
my skin and tease
the longing of
my heart…

then I would see
you standing there;
the morning colors
in your hair.
Forgive me if
I'm unaware
of others
standing near.

Dingle Day
poems by Joe O'Connell

Music-energy

In Flanders fields
Did Bob Seeger and the Silver Bullet Band
Buoy us up on a Spring morning
With a driving force,
Ebullient, hoarse and sound,
Prophetic energy about nothing much really
Or everything
That a young sub-prime man should feel,
The world and its promise wheeling under his heel.
In rushy Kerry fields, actually,
Were these musical propellers felt,
The sun winning supremely over the fluffy clouds
For attention received unsolicited
Like a fancied one,
Its power and beauty constant,
Immutable and impermeable to any move,
Indifferent to the machinations
Of an earth bound offspring.

Fair day

Garrulous he was
Obstreperous he was not.
From the hills he hailed,
Kerry cows and sheep he kept,
Solemnly tending,
Serenely cultivating
Bringing seed to mellow fruition.

Alone in person
But not alone in faith,
This, his infrequent occasion
To imbibe in good cheer
To his heart's content
No end of frothy black beer
From stout barrels sent.

With shout and song
Did he share stout
All day long
With those who sold
Or had nothing to sell
But were communed in fraternal unity.

Poetry to him was alien as wine,
But the flowing words exchanged
During the flow of urine
In the outhouse made
The music of gods
Sound like Morse code.

And the slap on the back
And the laughter, the cheer,
Rendered errant thoughts
Of returning to his abode

Like a bed unmade:
The time can wait
'Til the buoyancy swells
And the tides abate.

Lambs sent to the slaughterhouse
Sent him to the porterhouse,
Them to squeal their last;
Him to squeal in mirth
While the porter would last.

Aromas of pipe-smoke
And that of Woodbines
Accompanied those of beery breath
And boots unclean
From miry streets
Newly smeared
By cattle, sheep and unruly swine,
Brazen guests for a day
Of a reluctant town.

Topcoats musty
And damp with rain,
Shirts and fingers motley stained
With porter and nicotine.
Tales tall
And feats not small,
Of good deals and desperate

Were recounted in great confidence
From drooling mouth
To hairy ear.

While horses patient
Awaited further orders
And faithful sheepdogs in pub-siege laid
Urgent rounds were ordered.
Turf cutting was arranged
To fuel the trusty Stanley range.

The services of mighty bulls were secured
And the merits of a bevy
Of marriageable local ladies
Were considered
Amongst men whose ideal of a perfect wife
Would rarely be realized
During their natural
And land-tethered life.

This was it!
Jokes and witty commentaries,
Garrulous growling,
All ground to a hush
To accommodate the spirited rendition
Of lyrics rebellious and romantic,
Each and every pub-action suspended,
Apart from solemn utterances
Of approval and encouragement
Directed to the man,
Talented, primed or drunk enough
To give vent to the lyric and air,
Often lost,

But now swirling vividly,
Expressed without care
From a mind relieved from the habitual toil
And endless drudgery
Which has finally culminated
In bounteous revelry
And well-earned levity
At the March fair.

Halloevening

That fairies, or pucai, don't exist
In the glaringly obvious physical sense
Is utterly besides the point
To any celtically attuned
Consciousness
Centred and diffused
Through the pale, cold autumnal
Halloevening thin air
In damp, mushroomy, rushy fields
Amongst meditative bovines,
Mysterious sheep, wild-eyed goats
And furtive little beings,
Who, surprised, turn their independent eyes
Almost, yet somehow more than human,
Towards your questing,
Knowing something, arrogantly conveyed,
That your quest will never find.

Toward the Heliopause
by Joan Michelson

Lament

And are you gone from me?
And are you dead?
Who loved me always
and now prefer the wind.

And is it spring
with an untimely frost?
And are the bushes sticks?
And berry-flowers dew?

And do I waking wake?
And is this floor the earth?
And do I breathe in smoke?
And is this wind?

Oh are you not alive?
Who loved me as your own
and gave me seasons
buttered with the sun.

Song For Sleep

I sleep and hold your hand
and hold your hand in sleep.

A shrunken moon slides in.
The eucalyptus breathes.
The garden shed grows tall,
taller than the hedge.

And years roll on, roll on
until we have no years

Then like blossom floats
an alphabet of dust.
I hold in sleep your hand.
In sleep I hold your hand.

New poem from Joan Michelson

Bosnian Girl

When they had done with her and her mother
she climbed a tree and hung herself – a girl
in a red sweater that her mother had knitted.
This is one front page image I remember
from the Srebrenica massacre.
If we could live inside the memory of 'Once
there was a village that was undisturbed',
by now she'd be a mother knitting sweaters
for her own daughter. My fingers unbuckle
the woven belt she slung around a branch.
Her slim bare legs are swinging down.
Feet on earth again, up she springs and runs.

Black Kripple Delivers
Poetry & Lyrics by Leroy Franklin Moore, Jr. aka the Black Kripple

Little Boy of the Blues
(For the late Josh White Sr.)

Grew up on southern streets
Melody rocked him to sleep
He were the eyes for blind Bluesmen

Little Boy of Folk/Blues

Learned the tricks of the trade
Made sure that blind bluesmen got paid
He guided the best many said

Lemon Jefferson, John Henry Arnold, Joe Taggart, Blake
All requested
This Little Boy of Folk/Blues

"Mom, I'm going on the road!
I'll send money home."
"It was for the best" mom knew "he must go"

Had to show who was boss
Because they knew the streets were mean & cold
And no place for an innocent boy

Blind Bluesmen taught what they knew
Sang songs of survival
Kept their guard up to all people

Little Boy of Folk/Blues

Got a taste of tough love
On the brink of abuse
Lived grown men's blues

Had to do
What needed to be done
by any means

Tip-toed on Jim Crow
through mosquito heat & salty snow
to clubs that he knew he was too young to go

Slept with one eye open
He was chosen
This Little Boy of Folk/Blues

No space for mistakes
Avoided streams & lakes
Blind Bluesmen walked on his pathways

Carried a lot on his shoulders
No time to play
The road made him older

Little Boy of Folk/Blues
wore men suits
to get in places where he wasn't suppose to

Money & music
is what he thought he would receive
but he got a whole lot more

Stories filled up books
Told how crooks ripped off Blind Bluesmen
Songs spin on radio without them knowing

Little Boy of Folk/Blues

Is not a boy any more
Told his son about the road
Yesterday it was the Blues today its Hip-Hop

Sat alone old and gray
Singing his own Blues
Still waiting to receive his dues

Moan To Me

Intro
Mmmmmmm
Mmmmmmm

Verse 1
Moan to me no not my baby
Going back down to the Delta
In the air you hear them holla
Sweating in the southern humidity

Chorus
Black blind men on corners
Singing for their rent & dinner
Blind Willie Johnson moan to me
Wailing about Black reality

Verse 2
No lyrics no words
It's all about feelings
Free like a bird
But with no wings

Chorus
Black blind men on corners
Singing for their rent & dinner
Blind Willie Johnson moan to me
Wailing about Black reality

Bridge
Not one tear, Jim Crow fear
Michelle Alexander yeah it's still here
Let's all moan
Trying to connect with our cell phones

Verse 3
All we want is human touch
Is that asking too much?
Going back down to the Delta
News coming from the Blues, don't need media

Chorus
Black blind men on corners
Singing for their rent & dinner
Blind Willie Johnson moan to me
Wailing about Black reality

Verse 4
Blues women show Hip-Hop queens
How to get it done and work behind the scenes
Reveal to them who were really pulling the strings
On guitar and yeah we have come so far

Verse 5
Moan for me
Moan about the game we still have to play
Moan cause nothing has changed
Moan there are no words to say

Moan for me
Mmmmmmm
Mmmmmmm
Blind Willie Johnson moan to me

New poem from Leroy Moore

Brown Krips Holding & Becoming Internationally
(Dedicated to Brown Disabled People World-Wide)

Bolivia to Nigeria Brown Krips on camera
Black & Blue by popo all around the world
Erase by movements & mainstream media

Only $14, monthly benefits
4 years, here comes the Olympics
Moving us out from London to Rio

Once again here we go
Pulling out water hose
Took it to the bridge

Protesters pushing governments to the edge
Hanging from ropes
Disabled Bolivians internationlly giving Brown Krips hope

Gentrifying in the home of Hip-Hop
International stories from Krip-Hop
However oppression don't stop

Special education to prison now we are locked up
Institutionalize eating slop
Working on the streets selling art stuff

Calling our work begging
Through the hoops they have us jumping
US hospitals from LA to DC wheelchair dumping

World-wide we are more than just breathing
On social networks networking
Blogging and podcasting

Creating our own language, Afro-Krip
We were on the bottom of slave ships
Now we are giving our oppressors lip

All of this on a ssi benefit
We had to be woke
Before Eric Garner

Brown Krips have been choking
By the hands of police, policy makers & politicians
And nobody really paid attention

We keep on thriving
From our beds/cardboard houses
Holding & becoming

The Forgotten Shore
J. C. Linstroth

Wallowed

Wallowed?...
Wallowed in what?...
In sin? In shit?...
Pray tell, a crumb of stale bread, a sip of vinegar wine...
Where's the priest? Where's Godot?...
Rolling around in my own filth...
But it's mine and no one else's...
I heard the pig root in the garden again today...
I heard Mozart while throwing up again today...
A sparrow lay dead in the field covered in Dali's ants...
Does time wallow or melt?...
I watched black swallows rise and dive and rise and dive...
The air smelling heavy with rain...
Why not Hollowed? Borrowed? Swallowed (birds?)? Hallowed?
I saw a jade snake slowly begin eating birds' eggs, mouth extended, gullet distended...
What's left?...
And Buddha said nothingness and I was afraid to believe...
Only in star dust...
And the gloaming beyond my own eyes...

Picasso's Fragments

Her white scattered face with flayed fingers, ogling oval eyes, heavily lashed, star gazed…
Finger-nailed tears, yellow-golden jeweled tear…
Green disjointed nose, red mis-angled hat with jagged blue carnation…
A face split into two conjoined halves, yellow-green…
White chattering-teeth, flailing albicant fingers, green stubs, yellowed fingernails…
Streaming black-smalt hair…

A face of utter horror…
A face of absolute grief…
A terrorized disconcerting staring gaze…
A visage forever frozen and collapsing in on itself with imploding ivory digits…
Tremulous sickly niveous fingers and hands…

Is this what you look like in the mirror when you think of me?…
Are you indeed Dora Maar?…
No, otherwise I would hardly know you…

For I know these Sartrean fragments…
Your sadness in Kafkaesque relief…
Why do you weep so?…
Is it for me you wail?…
Or, is it for yourself bawling thus?…
Or, is it for us?…

For there is the us, which can never be…
Never more…
For how will I ever encompass all of your sorrow?…

I can never hope to ever envelop your terror and abject hate…
Do you loathe me so?…
Is this why you grieve?…
Am I not what you thought I was?…
Will your depression last forever?…

I may never be able to comfort or soothe thee as thou dost deserve…
For I am only mortal with all the frailty of humankind, and perhaps worse…
Stop torturing yourself my darling…
You will be alright…
I will be alright…
We will both of us journey onward…

Albeit never the same…

KATRINA
by Lyn Lifsin

It's Dark, it's Shirt-Soaking Hot

and the only word to
describe the heavy
odor is "indescribable."
Still, they refuse to leave.
Even the sight of corpses
tied to banisters to stop
them from drifting failed
to drive off straggling
New Orleans homeless.
Some finally say "I've
had enough." They're
running out of food.
There are human remains
in different houses. *The
smell messes with
your psyche.* One woman
stays so she can take
care of her parents
who are disabled. She
walks around waving a
white flag so no one
mistakes her for a looter

130 to 150 Bodies a Day

in the temporary mortuary

fingerprints, x rays, DNA.
After that officials
will turn the bodies
over to Louisiana officials
and then to the families

some bodies so decomposed
DNA will be the
only identification

MALALA
by Lyn Lifhin

On the Day Rushing to the Metro Already a Little Late on My Way to Ballet I Nearly Skid on Acrons, Catch Myself

I think of Malala, maybe rushing, never
wanting to think her name means "grief
stricken," as I've written a poem about
becoming what you're called. Maybe
she was humming a song she heard once
on TV before the Taliban banned it or
was watching leaves drift from the bus
or giggling with girl friends. Maybe
she was thinking of being a doctor and
coming back to treat young children
in her region, her swat. Or maybe she
was hoping to see a certain boy with
licorice eyes and a smile who always
made her giggle. No longer able to wear
school uniforms, told to wear plain
clothes, Malala wrote in her blog,
Instead, I decided to wear my favorite
pink dress. Maybe the last beautiful
thing she saw as the bullet entered her
mahogany curls until later she woke
up in the hospital's cone of light

Malala Dreams of Military Helicopters

no longer throwing
toffee from the sky
but filling the air
with darkness. She
could hear artillery
fire. By morning
half the girls kept
coming to school.
On her way home
she heard a man say
"I will kill you."
It sounded like a
requiem. Withered
leaves fell thru
her hair as if she
was still dreaming.
Dark birds of her
dreams plunging
in flame on to hill
sides that once
looked as if they'd
been dipped in beauty

New poems on Syria by Lyn Lifshin

The Last Garden in Aleppo

this small oasis of color and life
as cluster bombs, barrel
bombs, missiles rain on houses,
hospitals, schools in this
hazardous, unpredictable place,
a gardener was able to grow
flowers, vegetables, broad
leaved plants. Roses, gardenias,
bougainvillea. The gardener's
whole existence dedicated
to the beauty of life, a small
courageous attempt to promote
peace. Dust and smoke blur
the stars, the watered ferns and
lilies in the shadows. Shivering
thru the raids, dreaming of
his dead wife until eventually a
barrel bomb lands near his
garden, kills him, his dream that
the "essence of the world is a
flower," the color, smell, how it
can inspire. But in the time
since his death, Aleppo seems
mostly defined by another
floral attribute: fragility

In Aleppo, a Haven of Beauty

in the middle of
hell on earth. But
it was more than
the jade abundance
and the brilliant
colors that made it
an oasis of tranquility
and repose for those
who chose to stay
in Aleppo or can't
leave. Barley wind
from Yarmook River.
Abu Ward, whose name
means "father of the
flowers," fought to
preserve beauty in the
rubble of what has
been from the
last remaining garden
center in the once
bustling liberated area
of Aleppo. "My place
is worth billions of
dollars," he told
a video journalist, "it
soothes like Mozart."

Of One and Many Worlds
Buddhist poems by Rayn Roberts

Of One and Many Worlds
> I dwell in Possibility— Emily Dickinson

Where winter ends and spring begins
white plum willow green
yellow broom
break the monotony
of brown and grey
magnolias open like hands
asking nothing
offering all
Beak wing and claw
gather twig cloth limb and stick
whatever warms
the magpie nestling
In the waking hills
feral cats hunt and fatten
A white haze of mountain sky
falls to earth
foggy breath of an imperial dragon—
There is meaning
in every motion or change
the momentary violets
pushing into light, are questions
the old trap of time letting go—
Is the coming of joy
and more pain
worth the space I take,
is the choice free
I don't know, but hold as seasons
spin 'round
this eternal spring
waking a world to all that is possible

Each Morning Begins a Journey
Until You Arrive At Who You Are

Out in the yard, one big palm stands in the sun.
Though it knows the secret of creating dates
How pigeons, new eggs in nest
Keep deep in shadow
Out of heat and rain
How to lean in the wind and not break
It mostly knows the passage of time.

A woman is raking the lawn in the palm shade.
Her two boys lean out a high window
Of the two-story government house
Dangling arms
Dropping bread to blackbirds below
Red-flecked wings
Yellow eyes in heads that tilt as they walk.

There is no sound but the birds, no meaning
To their jagged song but joy, no clothes for boys
But flannel pajamas.
The woman is the Mother of a World
And everywhere it is always Sunday morning—
As a younger man, father was a jeweler
Had to leave that trade to fight the Japanese

Won medals, got promoted, remained a Marine
It is 1953; he is killing Chinese and Koreans
In a world of craters
Broken trees, bombed out villages

Children starving in the dark, old men eating rats—
The palm moves in dry air; the birds peck the bread,
The woman sweeps up the remaining leaves, the boys

Pull on jeans and continue their journey to manhood.

Poetic Matrix Press

New poems by Rayn Roberts

Lament for the Body Politic

You are better to believe what we tell the children, God loves all,
Satan's to blame for the evil in the world, the horror of war.
You're better if you just think it, think the heart of humanity
The soul of the nation is one, indivisible under Donald J.
Oh say can you see something eating away at the heart-land
Like an amoeba eatin' the brain, a crow peckin' the liver of liberty?
Chipping away inside, Death has a bone to pick with all of us
We let hate and war go over and over but never have we
Quite committed to memory how we do it— books rust on shelves
Our art rots on walls, movies distracted us like football
Our laws help check but there is no remedy for reality— Violence
Erupts at any turn, with or without imams, rabbis, or priests
A merciful God almighty Wall Street— No gettin' out of it til we
Lay down our views, our arms and teach the kids peace—
Believe that's possible and you're better than me, pushin' seventy
Kickin' the tires on heavenly car, never seen nothin' like it so far.

Reminiscence

Fishing at the river, some boys jump in
Swim across and back so quickly
It makes my head spin.
If I were trim and lean like them, I'd go in.
I did when I was that age
Set down my rod
Shed my clothes
Took to any lake or stream
Swam my sweaty body clean
Lay on the bank and dreamed of love—
But I am old now, these days
I need prodding
Just to take a bath!
A boy needs no prod, only doing
Without hesitation or regret
Sagacious are the old men, but wisdom
Does not come
Unless the joys of youth are done
And as the mind goes under, we learn to swim.—

The Unequivicality of a Rose
by Joel Netsky

As the Explorer

As the explorer, agape, peregrinated in the land,
only in the abstract could his mind plant there
the institutions of his native country and streets.

Suddenly, with certitude proximal to the demonstrative,
he clasped that what would take root of those
institutions there,
that what takes root of institutions anywhere,
is the universal in them:
there was a law of life - invisible, immutable -
which governed, that was as omnipresent as the air.

At Glance

    At glance he was loof, yet his nature was but contemplative: surely before the construct is its cogitate. To him, what lay exterior the walls of the universe was a question so fraught that the prodigious deeds of logic existed solely to champion the answer

A teacher,
"Be not so obdurate upon yourself.
Is the soul not a receptacle into which one should pour
        oneself
no differently than tea into a cup?"

    Her voice planted the quiet affection.

"Is the soul a citadel, that it be beseiged,
or in distant orb, that one travel interminably?"

    Into her tea she gazed. Its calm led her down steps in the side of the cup until she was standing on the bottom. She added honey - how fragrant the inhale!

"Is the soul not a receptacle into which one should
       pour oneself
no differently than tea into a cup?"

Realization Point
by Chris Hoffman

Handies Peak

When the whole mountain
lies under your feet,
put there with leg muscle
and deep breathing,
you begin to see
what the mountain sees—
distances expanding
through the polished air,
the steep falling away
from this high reach
of rock and talus with its scabs
of orange and gray-green lichen,
the trickles of sky water from snowfields
and, far down, the brief summer flourish
of alpine meadows, and farther yet
and wide away rolling on and on
the velvet blanket of the forest
to a narrow yellow band of lowland
curving at the horizon.

Like a cone of seeds,
under one of those numberless trees
lies your bundle of daily cares,
whereabouts unknown.

You see daylight and drifting cloud shadows
play across the undulant land
like a blessing
for the largeness of life
and a tap on the shoulder
for the shortness of days.

Oasis

On this clear night
a small watch fire is flickering
and waving its tendrils of spicy smoke
beside the well in the inner courtyard.

Your host has served you
lamb with pilaf and sweet tea
and now you are alone in the late hours,
within these four sturdy walls,
watching the stars swing imperturbably
as they have for generations.

A meteor strikes like a match across the sky.
From somewhere, muted by the distance,
comes the music of a lute
and the rhythm of hands on a drum skin.

Looking back on the long journey
it seems the days were beaded on a string
that led inevitably here,
though at the time most were just an effort
to discover how to do one's best,
and some just felt like failure.
But now the gems of days stand out.

And now the name of names
forms on your lips,
not to attain or ask for anything,
but simply in gratitude
and to participate in the flowing forth of life;
for nothing is ever completed,
only renewed.

New poem by Chris Hoffman

Advice from the Last Loon

If you heard my cry even once
when you were young
you still have not forgotten

that sudden wild sweet pang of yearning
now born inside you for a paradise
you had not even known existed.

I know what it is like to rest on a pillow
of blue water twinkling with sunstars,
with my youngster on my back
and my partner beside me.

I know the immutable dark green of the pines
and have seen stark winter branches
unfurl each spring their buds of green flame
into an amazement of foliage
mad to sort the winds of any summer storm.

I know that joy takes many forms.

I know cold rain
and moody mornings
when the air hangs thick with mists.

I know the long dive in clear clean water
and the skill of the catch
and the satisfaction of feeding one's constant companion,
hunger.

And in my many lives
I have known the closing of the eye
and have felt the teeth of fox
pierce my body.

I know the utter stillness of deep nights
far removed from human commotion.

And I have seen when colder days
splash burning reds and startling yellows
over my neighbors, the hills.

All of this, my life,
I put into my cry.

And, as I am the last of my kind,
I make this request:

Carry my cry with you
as you travel through desperate times
into the future, as in
your many stories of an ark
carrying life safely through a flood.

What my cry has touched in you
is the source of your gift.

Live my cry
when you work to heal the world.

River Light
Chris Olander

Comets

Five days after
Yosemite Valley reopens—
river's beautiful devastation
reclaiming the old ways
in a ripple through an era's tide—
April Christens the valley:
indigo clouds fuel sunset
rain veils' fire.
Granite ignites!

The day's last light gone.
Drive home through dark
canyon shapes curve up mountain
around ridge rock—over
into forest enclosure—
down—blind turn—

Enormous!
Canyon black void opens.
Strange tint of moonlight rising
behind Sierras coronas crest line crystal.
The bright comet flares northwest
perfect above horizon—soon gone!
Never again in our lives—
How can we value that
in wondrous lights of space?

To comfort lack in immensity
dropping into canyon, steep, dark
narrow winding road, pull off slow

onto shoulder at cliff edge—stop!
Turn off headlights, engine, set brake.

Soon, full moon over the ridge
above us.
We step into galactic star fire—
Breathe the cool breeze—moist.

Meteor streak!
Hidden moon—strange glow silvering
ridge lines etching before us—
Tuolumne—Stanislaus—American.
What value this space we share?

Cliff edge falls into river's rush-roar
muffles millions of years carving deeper—
dark around us—no human light—
balmy whispers cliff chaparral—

The comet's crystal veil
blessing Andromeda and Perseus
guiding us home among these stars—
atoms of a universe—
swirling our Milky Way flesh—
Warm with each other
loving one another
breathing the wind's ridge pines—
the full moon rising—eclipsed!
In black pearl glow we kiss—

Blue Earth

Granite slabs
    avalanche the crystals'
        ecstatic laughter—-
basalt's liquid tongues
    cascade the cliff's teeth

and the Sierra's red earth
    marbles blue stone veins
        to ocean's heart beat

fire rippling the wilderness
    and the waves' flames
        leap from the prophet's tongue
as sand rivulets sift shapes
    pattern the landscape's brilliance

the watershed's flesh
    channels stone into blue clay
        shaping our vessel's worth.

Finding Passage
Molly Weller

On Finding Myself on the Map

The map lies stretched out
sleek against the cushions of the couch
light winking on its laminate.
Yellow roads scurry
over its surface,
popping out from a backdrop
of pale parks
and white-striped neighborhoods.
Glebe Island Bridge in blue
twists around one corner
through Darling Harbour
then races off the top edge
only pausing for a breath
at the Cahill Expressway.
Boxy Moore Park rounds out
into a bulbous Centennial
then slims
following Darley to the Queens.
I sit on a lower corner
hardly on the map
but there, perched
left butt cheek
covering the train station marker
a pink square
right off City Road
the noise from passing cars
vibrating its windows.

Quilter's Burden

The table trembles on hollow legs
hinged at the middle like a knee,
bent against the weight.
Piles of cloth
lean on each other in exhaustion.
The creamy top bows and sags
strewn like the floor beneath
with half-finished projects.
An iron stands commanding,
chest puffed with dignity
defying comment on its limp cord.
A backpack, lifeless and empty
lies still across the cutting mat.
The spool, wound tight in a navy shade,
stands pricked
by a single needle,
its empty eye
looking darkly at the room.

New poems by Molly Weller

Jornada del Muerto

Southwest of the heart's heart, midway to gut sense,
a specter string ties man to the red earth,
binding all to weather, water, change.
The Great Blue Sky bends a theatrical arc above dry land,
its impressionist cloudscape an excess on the high, hot desert face.
Silt streams silent winds across cracked gypsum mudflats,
pooling on the spiny limbs of *Ephedra torreyana*.
Clumps of *Sporobolus nealleyi clutch the earth in sparse rings*.
No cacti loom ancestral ghosts for shade or amnesty.
No pink flower softens the landscape,
nor opens flimsy petals to the rising moon.
A tug, the land upon man, draws him down,
like a drop of rain on the bleached, bone dry earth.

Apple Orchard

We have lost the art of apple growing;
forgotten to run pigs in the orchards,

forgotten to plant the trees facing east,
where the first rays of sun can lift the morning dew,

forgotten to thin the spurs to plump the fruit.
So much lost. Lost the card catalog. Lost the recipe box

handed down from mother to daughter;
a battered metal lid hiding the perfume of family dinners.

We have lost the need to remember
the authority of ages past.

No need for the rememberers,
for the storytellers, for the Wise Man.

The wise men are forgotten
and the apples.

LISTENING: NEW & SELECTED WORK
by Charles Entrekin

Hay Stacker

     Too small to lift a pitch fork full from
below, I would climb up top and catch each throw,
mid-air, then guide and drop the load in one motion,
until the wagon would hold no more.
     Then coming out of the dust from the back four acres
I'd be atop the hay, barely able to breathe in the heat,
yet lying back in the wet of my own sweat, almost complete.
     And when we passed beneath the big pear tree
there in the middle of my grandfather's pasture,
I knew how it would be:
I would stick out my hand and
take the pear straight out of the air,
without effort; it would come to me
because it belonged to me.
     I hadn't yet guessed how things could go wrong,
or how it might be to be left alone, or that one
could lose badly and go down at the end
like my mother, shaking and defeated.
     I was, in that moment, simply there
watching my cousins and uncles in the distance, shimmering
in the hot air like mirages in black rubber boots,
with pitch forks in hand,
     and when I took my first dusty bite,
     it was like my first
sinking deep into a woman's body,
almost overwhelming, and I could feel
     the pear's juice sinking into me
as I lay there in the hay-scented air, adrift
and becoming everything around me,
     until suddenly I laughed out loud
     without knowing

what the laughter was about
as it poured out of me
at the top of the tree-high stack
while the future waited,
and I was carried on the harvest to the barn.

Day After the Market Crash
San Francisco, October, 1987

The spare change
saxophone player
at Market and Sansome
holds sway over the pink
gray day, and five o'clock
faces in pin striped suits, and
a young man and his girl, sipping beer
beside the bank's imitation Greek patio,
its concrete columns roofed with glass.

As if in a dream, his sound comes from
inside a cacophony of commuters at day's end,
from all the transients in this corner of the city,
the weaselly newspaper vendor, the birdlike
yelps and yells of bicycle messengers, their
punk reed hair, warlike warnings subtly fading
into air, as suddenly from inside it all,
the spare change saxophone player blows, leaning back,
knees bent, eyes closed, into the hollow of the bank's
echoes. A Mississippi melody.
A sound of innocence lost,
echoes.

The Art of Healing
by Charles Entrekin & Gail Rudd Entrekin

Forgiveness

Lost in the shuffle
the present seems far away,
like the whisper of tires in the rain,
like the voice of whippoorwill
summers past, like the light
of stars gone dead but still shining
in this incipient night.
The timer above the stove
will soon stop, its green glow
go red, will chime twice
and go silent.
There is no intent,
the Buddha's moon-faced mask
will remain fragmented
under the maple tree.
You don't have to fix it.

C

Nature Noir

        Safe in our Sierra Nevada
cool mountain breeze, listening to the
hot tub bubbling around us, we lie back
pink in the last of the daylight,
watch a pale green praying mantis
strike a tai-chi pose, become a twig
an uninvolved stick,
a part of a leaf on the deck,
        and then as I'm about to speak
it happens:
the mantis, nature's ninja,
blurs like a film in fast forward,
snags a black bumblebee from flight,
drags it to a sudden stop.
        But then the counter movement of life
swirls before the death bite,
and I watch the diaphanous wings
pull free.
        And as the black bee takes the air,
something inside me sees
a second chance,
the life I have not yet lived.

C

Chronic Lymphocytic Leukemia

When the monster grabbed him up, tossed him back
into its mouth, we had been swimming along holding hands
and I didn't let go, flew up dripping and dropped beside him
into the dark and foreign place where there were others
dimly swimming for their lives and there were teeth that grazed
our skins now and then as we lay very still, our hope ballooning,
rising up into the sinuses of the creature intermingled
with our fear so that both rose equally and were, we prayed,
equally compelling, but the truth, we knew, was that the beast
was dumb and barely knew we were there.
                                                          Every day
it tested its spikes against our naked fragile bodies,
some days teasing us by tipping forward, almost letting
us roll out into the frothy sea, but most days we lay still,
read medical books, listened to the messages of friends
sending love and encouragement from far away places
where life went on in warm kitchens and the linens
were clean and dry.
                            Finally, the thing decided not to decide,
let us wash out with the tide. We are swimming again
and the ocean is very blue. But there is a fin moving
beside us on the horizon and though it disappears
from time to time in the bright sun
at dusk it is always there
circling.

G

Before Making Love

Finally, we tell the truth: how death's been
hovering at the door, muttering threats and banging
in the long night, how reason takes flight
like a circling falcon over its nest of flapping
fear, how you sometimes wander out into the ocean fog,
how I am so angry I cannot speak, that you
who took the vow, would drift down the beach
accept the icy water, leave me to lift the heavy boat
lock the oars, paddle the hard night, looking
for you; leave me to rake the sand,
build the park, martial the troops, while
you stand down there, your pant legs sloshing
in the water, smiling at the crows,
not helping, not helping at all
with the work of life, just because
you are leaving soon. And I don't want
this version of myself. I want to fall
adrift beside you, am terrified that I
will fall adrift beside you, that the two
of us will wade out into the cold
grey sea. And I don't want this version
of you, timid and silent, waiting to be told
bumping along tipping and spilling the wine,
the vase, my words. Nor this version of us
still in the same story but no longer
the protagonists, the lovers, the driving nexus
of the plot, only separate wanderers, rarely
found on the same page. Give me back
the glittering scarf, the ready laughter,
the bodies that twine in the night.

G

Change (will do you good)
by Gail Rudd Entrekin

Blue Whales

Blue whales are out there somewhere,
six thousand of the hundreds of thousands
that once roamed the planet's seas.
Now separated from each other
by thousands of miles, they moan their loneliness
four octaves below middle C, so low, so slow,
we humans cannot even hear. But on our ocean liners
and in our lighthouse kitchens, the cutlery jangles on the table,
the glass pane vibrates in its frame, and we know
something nearby is crying out in need.
Two thousand miles away, they can be heard
and answered, the loudest sound made by a living thing,
and we don't know what it says, but only that,
speeded up ten times, what we hear is a long, blue,
unearthly note, a gurgle so deep
we slip down into our own lostness,
grateful that they are carrying for us
something bigger than we could hold.

Snoring

Not like at the hostel
where the old man's snorts and gurgles
burst forth erratically, always preceded
by a brief silence for maximum
explosive effect, so that sleep
came to us in small increments
broken again and again by his desperate
gasps and bombastic ejaculations of air
until we all gave up sleep and lay
furious in the dark
considering pillows over his face,
almost anything for an hour of peace.

No, this snoring, rhythmic and reliable,
I have hitched my dreaming to for 20 years,
linked my own breath to a more powerful machine
and let myself be towed
through the mysterious sea of night
the way the boys on our street
used to catch the wind behind a fast car
down Franklin Blvd., their bikes
flying in its wake,

the way my brother and I, down to our last dollar,
drove the interstate home in winter,
our dad dying in his bed,
our VW Beetle rusted full of holes,
no heater, and packed in blankets,
winter hats and gloves, we'd find a safe pocket

of wind behind a massive cargo truck
and draft the long cold night
snow sparkling in our headlights
like magical, untouchable dreams
and sail safely home to morning.

REARRANGEMENT OF THE INVISIBLE
by Gail Rudd Entrekin

Rearrangement of the Invisible

And here he comes again, that querulous old man
with his pointy hat, his knobby walking stick,
curl-toed shoes, pulling behind him the next installment
of your life, whether you're ready or not,
sweeping ahead in his push broom the scraps
and shards of your story so far —

Just as you were getting used to the white roses,
those blowsy blooms along the edges of the lawn,
the doe steps delicately out of the dark
while you're sleeping, incises every bud,
every blossom, leaving naked sticks piercing
the night, and despite the dog throwing herself
against the door, by the time you push it open,
stagger out in your threadbare nightshirt,
the deer has slipped away like a ghost
into the woods beyond the pointless fence.

You wake in the morning to a whole new landscape,
and when you cry out, wringing your hands and cursing,
the dog sits down and fixes you in her patient gaze —
she tried to tell you (but you wouldn't wake up)
that the old man was passing down the road
rearranging your future, and the thing growing
in your bones, which won't be identified for weeks,
is the seed of a whole new order.

Something Coming

We are beginning to understand something
of what is coming, to go beyond sensing a shadow
in the woods watching us, and to see it take shape,
see it coming toward us across a field, zigzagging
as it does, now standing idle and watching the sky,
now heading directly for us at a trot. And realizing
that we are seen, that it will find us no matter
what we do, we are slowing down.
                                                    We are
standing very still hoping to blend with the waving
greens of this raw springtime, to stay downwind
of it as warmer breezes pick up and buffet the leaves,
the grasses, tossing everything in a moving salad
of life; we sway on our legs, trying to move with the air
that surrounds us, and we stop thinking of what is around
the next bend in the path, stop planning our next
escape route, and begin to merge with the moment;
we have slipped into a painting by Van Gogh;
something is coming again across the fields and we
are open as sunflowers in full bloom
to these last moments on the earth.

New poems by Gail Rudd Entrekin
(for Charles on his 74th birthday)

Blue Moon
(the second full moon in a given month, occurring about every 2 ½ years)

and which isn't blue, but pearly as an abalone disc
washed ashore above the roof tops.
Just before bed we shuffled out in our slippers and night clothes,
in time to see it break free above the tree line
almost bouncing as the trees relinquished it,
settled back into their quiet places
empty handed. I helped you find it, that flood
of light, with your broken eyes,
and we stood there swaying with the trees
marveling.

At the last blue moon we must have been
learning to stand to the newest loss,
your cancer finally behind us, and the Parkinson's,
your dis-integrating vision waiting in the wings.
At the next one, for all we know we may be gone,
nothing but a memory, and so I yipped a tentative yip,
and then you yipped back in your crumbly voice
that gives way a bit, falls back, and then
my voice began to fill out, lift into a howl
and then, neighbors be damned,
another howl for both of us rose up,
round and full of all the lost and broken things,
lifted up in my chest, poured out of my throat
and the long high note spun
all that loss into silver light.

Nepenthe

At the restaurant on the coast, having survived
three flights of stone steps to sit at the counter
along the rail on the top deck, we are overlooking
the vast blinding brightness of the sea.
I am stunned by the effort it has taken, the lack
of transcendence in the resulting bustle
of ordinary eating and serving. We share
a pulled pork sandwich, a slice of apple pie.
We are mostly silent now. Our effort
to be cheerful has washed us empty and clean.

Finally we stand to go, gather our jackets, bags,
his slender new cane. As he comes along carefully
avoiding the tables, the feet, I stand watching
the water far below jostle and swell in its enormous
bowl, and he joins me, turns back to the view.
Is it mountains? He asks. After a moment
I take his arm. We turn. We walk away.

In A Dress Made Of Butterflies
poems by Sandra Lee Stillwell

Seeing Coyote

I emerge from the garden
in the half dark of a sodden December day
in time to see a late flock of geese
high above the mirrored grey of the bay.

In the peripheral I see a shadow
move out of the bull rushes
and into the open.
It is Coyote,
seen lately trotting along the trails
that caress the curve of water's edge.

No more than a silhouette
in the lost light of another day,
I cannot see his face
but I am confident that he sees all of me.

My instincts have waned,
evolved away from the basic urge to feed myself,
to survive and now are bent around a clock
that binds me to a paycheck.

His instincts are raw, real.
He follows the rules of his world,
stays on the edge of my life, lest I harm him.
He eats only that which cannot eat him.

I stare into the space where he was
wondering what it feels like to trudge through the
wet,
hungry and knowing
this is the life you've been given,
wondering, is that so bad?
Am I so different?

I want to answer…
No, no.

In A Dress Made Of Butterflies

   In a dress made of butterflies
you dance at dawn
to a melody rich
with the voice of a dove,
or is it an old man's flute?

   The song
declares your life perennial,
infinite, eternal.

   As the sun begins to rise
and the moon slips away,
the sky grows dark with wild geese
winging their way
from cold, clear ponds
to fields full of ripening grain.
When they pass
the day is filled with the golden
yellow of a new morning,
and all the while you dance,
feet moving faster and faster,
your movements governed
by joy.

   You dance on and on,
until, with a sudden and final twirl,
you stop.
The butterflies
that make up your dress,
fly away in the sunlit day,

and there you stand, head bowed,
so innocent
that I am sure you do not know
you are naked.

      I move silently away
so as not to disturb your peace,
your prayer,
confident I will again watch you
dance at dawn
in a dress made of butterflies.

New poem by Sandy Lee Stillwell

For Mouska

She rests on my lap,
sides rise and fall
With each breath.
She is calm.

It was a long ride
for one so old.

She saw it all.
Smelled the acrid
black and purple smoke,
Saw the burning buildings,
homes,
trees exploding into flame,
felt the oven hot swirling winds
and heard the fast approaching roar
the crackle
of an angry fire.

In her sleep she stirs,
quivers,
cries out.

It may be that her dreams,
like mine,
take her back
to the little yellow house,
remind her of what is gone,
of what may come again.

She yearns
for the familiar,
wants to taste the sweet grass
of home,

rest in the speckled shade
of the lilac,
take in the pine scented air.

I want to open
the long gone screen door,
hear again it's squeaky hinges,
stroll past the cosmos,
allysum, marigolds, lobelia
and golden yarrow
to find her resting there
in that place she loved
between the white rose
and the bending lilac.

I want.

Winds of Change/Vientos de Cambio
bilingual poems by Tomás Gayton

Winds of Change (English)

Winds of change blow through corridors
of time and color
Doors open and close on an empty room
filled with memories
leading to the grave and beyond
The serpent's fang conceived in sin
of slavery
draws blood in midnight Mississippi heat
A brown baby scrambles into the comfort
of his parents' bed
On a steep Seattle hill he sleeps and
dreams, doors open and close
winds come and go, roses bloom in snow
Fleeing winter wind and spring rain
yellow canary wings his way
to warmer clime
beyond corridors of time and color

Vientos de Cambio (Spanish)

Los vientos de cambio soplan por corredores
de tiempo y de color
Las puertas se abren y se cierran en un cuarto vacío
lleno de recuerdos
que llevan a la tumba y al más allá
El colmillo de serpiente concebido en el pecado
de la esclavitud
extrae sangre en el calor de Mississippi a la medianoche
Un bebé moreno busca el calor
del lecho de sus padres
En una alta ladera de Seattle duerme y sueña—
puertas que se abren y cierran
vientos que van y vienen, rosas que florecen en la nieve
Escapando viento invernal y lluvia primaveral
el canario amarillo revolotea hacia
climas más calientes
más allá de los corredores de tiempo y color

Bahia (English)
(Dedicated to the Beautiful Baianas)

The girls of Bahia
take my breath away
as they swing and sway
to the beat of Condomblé[1]
I keep coming back
to sun and sand
to swim in the bay
and sip quaraná[2]
Bronze black bodies
bounce soccer balls
on swaying hips
The girls of Bahia
take my breath away
as they swing and sway
to the beat of Condomblé
Butterflies
flash and fly
on cresting waves
Bahian sun sets to
rhythm of drums
whistle of wind
The girls of Bahia
take my breath away
as they swing and sway
to the beat of Condomblé

---

[1] Syncretic religion of Brazil, incorporating Yoruba and Catholic influences
[2] Brazilian soft drink

Bahia (Spanish)
(Poema dedicado 'as belas baianas)

As meninas da Bahia
tiram todo o meu folego
quando andam e balançam
ao ritmo do Candomblé
Eu vivo voltando
ao sol e 'a areia
para nadar na baia
e tomar guaraná
Em corpos dourados
as bolas de futebol se movem
nas cinturas requebrantes
As meninas da Bahia
tiram todo o meu folego
quando andam e balançam
ao ritmo do Candomblé
Borboletas
brilham e voam
ondas se quebram
No por do sol baiano
no ritmo dos tambores
no assobio do vento
As meninas da Bahia
tiram todo o meu folego
quando andam e balançam
ao ritmo do Candomblé

Sojourn on the Bohemian Highway
by Tomás Gayton

Mexico's Forgotten Negros (excerpt)

One day while wandering around El Zócalo I meet Juan, a fair-complexioned mestizo owner of a travel agency in San Cristóbal de Las Casas, Chiapas. I ask him about the former slave chapel of San Nicolas behind the Cathedral just across from his office on El Zócalo. Juan's response, "Tomás, there have never been any black slaves in San Cristóbal." I open my journal and read to him the words I copied from the historical notice posted at the entrance to the chapel.

> *Alrededor de 1615, el obisbo Juan de Zapata y Sandoval fundó la ermita de San Nicolas de los Morenos para la confradía negra de Nuestra Señora de la Encarnación, la cual, en contra de lo acostumbrado en el caso de iglesias para negros y mulatos, se hizo en el centro de la ciudad. Fue el primer templo formal de la ciudad.*

> (Around 1615 the bishop Juan de Zapata y Sandoval founded the hermitage of San Nicolas of the dark ones for the confraternity of Our Lady of the Incarnation, which, contrary to custom in the case of churches for Negroes and mulattos, he placed in the center of the city. It was the first formal temple of the city.)

Juan, an intelligent man who once lived in La Jolla, California, still insists that, "There never were any negros in San Cristóbal." Juan's disturbing response is, regrettably, all too typical and misinformed. Africans were brought to Mexico 500 years ago as slaves to replace the indigenous population decimated by Spanish conquest and disease. Blacks have been in Mexico ever since, though their presence has been virtually ignored and underestimated until recent times.

"The Black population is not well known," says Sagrario Cruz, anthropology and history professor at the University of Veracruz, which offers the multidisciplinary program, Africa en México. She has documented distinct populations of slaves, maroons, black Seminoles and U.S. blacks, both free people and runaway slaves, who settled in the country before and after Mexico abolished slavery. Free blacks have lived in Mexico since as early as 1609. The two generals who led Mexico's war of independence from Spain, José María Morelos and Vicente Guerrero, after Father Hidalgo was executed by the Spanish in 1811, were of African ancestry. "El Negro Guerrero" was the second president of Mexico and he abolished slavery in 1829.

Henry Louis Gates, Jr.'s book and television documentary, Black in Latin America along with two other documentaries from Mexico, The Forgotten Roots and African Blood, recount the strong African heritage that has endured centuries of neglect in Mexico. These works show most Afromestizos or Afro-Mexicans are concentrated in the state of Veracruz on the Gulf Coast and in the states of Guerrero and Oaxaca on La Costa Chica (the Little Coast). La Costa Chica is a 200-mile long Pacific coastal region that begins just south of Acapulco and ends in Puerto Angel, Oaxaca. Together with Chiapas, they make up the three poorest states in Mexico.

In Veracruz, on the Caribbean coast, African culture and heritage persist most strongly in dance, music and song. They even have a museum celebrating Mexico's African heritage. However, on the Pacific Coast, African culture and tradition have been largely forgotten and lost to posterity.

New poem by Tomás Gayton

Why Do Black Lives Matter?

When every day we see them lost
By Legal Lynching
Easy targets for "Law Enforcement"
And the press to Stigmatize and Demonize
Because of our color

Why? I wonder
Must we relive Americaa's bloody history
of Slavery, Black Codesand Jim Crow
With daily accounts of Legal Lynching
In this New Century
Why do Black Deaths matter?

DRIVEN INTO THE SHADE
Brandon Cesmat

Driven Into the Shade

One Saturday morning after their divorce,
my dad drove home in a new Ford Maverick for Mom.
My little brothers were inside watching "The Bugs Bunny-Roadrunner Show."
I was in the driveway, watching Mom
hang her clothes on a pole above the back seat as if
each dress were one of her possible lives.
Dad pulled me under the oak at the side of the driveway
where the leaves' spindles jabbed my feet.
"Don't cry," he said. "Now she can get some rest."

> When we came home from school, we often found her lying down,
> the curtains drawn. Her back hurt, she said.
> The .22 pistol under her mattress kept her awake like a princess.
> This woman who had gentled horses and carried king snakes off the road
> wept daily. Her medication, she said, made her emotional.

Now wearing sunglasses, Mom carried her make-up case to the car.
She saw me in the shade with Dad and said,
"You said you'd take the kids from me. Now you have them."
I threw my arms around her legs so she couldn't walk.
I wanted to make them stay, but I made her say,
"Don't make this hard," and I made her pull my arms off her,
I felt her need to leave, and it was stronger than me.
She said, "I'm no good anymore."
The sand where she stood burned my feet.

> Two weeks before, we had passed Dad driving up the road;
> she swerved at him and said, "If you kids weren't in the car—"

Now Dad would be safe with us but
Mom was leaving, so when she went in the house for her purse,

I jumped into the car and locked the doors.
The keys swung in the ignition.
My father told me to open the door.

I shook my head *no*,
my reflection on the glass over his face.
"You're going to get spanked," he said.
I was no good, whole family no good:
Bad Dad, Bad Mom, Bad Boy.
Mom came out and told him to break the new car's window.
"My gun is in there."
Why would I want her gun? For that moment,
I brought my parents back together outside her new car.
Dad sighed and lifted a chunk of granite from along the drive.
Mom looked at me. With the windows up, the car had grown hot.
I said, I'd turn the key and touched the ignition,
but instead of holding them there, I made her turn
on him and say, "You almost had me, almost had my kids."
Dad dropped his stone, and stepped back, his face already blurring
                                                in my memory.

I knew my mother despised his lust for other women and
I was to hate that part of him and never be unfaithful.
Again he walked down the road and I told Mom to go indoors.
Outside the windshield and behind her sunglasses, she began to cry again
and promised not to spank me or drive away.
She held out her arms and asked me to open the door.
                      I was inside the glass.
                      I was eleven years old.
                      I had the gun and her medicine bottles.
                      I had the keys to a new car
                      pointed down the driveway, but
                      that moment to leave came too early for me.
I would not open until she went indoors.

One night years later, I drove along a valley above Provo
and swallowed the Quaaludes a woman gave me.
She had calm brown eyes.
We sipped tequila and orange juice while she told me her screenplay
about a woman who works her way home playing soprano saxphone.
I told her a story about a boy trapped in a car.
She laughed and pulled me out into a field where I remembered that

after my father walked around the curve in the road,
I unlocked the Maverick's door and
stepped onto the sandy driveway. My feet burned,
but cool air stung my lungs and the light off the leaves winked
as I ran for the shade.

The Long Pass

On the football field, some fight, others run away
after the long pass. For all the shoulder pads' clatter and
helmets' crack, football is less culturalistic Darwinism than
a complicated game of catch.

People who love me have always done so in spite of my desire
to hit and shove with or without pads, on grass or sand or mud
as long as the light holds,
                      the light necessary not to illuminate
the lineman who could dance like a dozen sumo wrestlers in the dark.
We light stadiums because football is a game of sky.

When I played tight-end—a halfway-house position for lapsed
                                              pacifists—
most of the game I would swing my forearms, throw my shoulders,
and drive my legs into the man across from me.
I was yell, muscle, grunt and rumble.

But for a few plays, I would release from the line and run downfield,
trying to put distance between myself and everyone. It felt good to be
                                              alone and
hope the ball would fall over my shoulder, into my hands, as soft
as I could make them, hold on tightly and run as far as possible.

For all the yelling, I learned to listen for football's quiet.
The long pass flies silently, is no "bomb" unless dropped.

The long pass is a prayer with answers

After the ball's snap,
the charge of the line, and
calls to put the quarterback in a sack,
                        the spinning oblong sphere brings a hush.
                            So much can go wrong between
                                  your hands and mine.

The linemen lean back from one another as the ball reaches the apex,
and even drunks in the bleachers quiet as the ball starts to drop
into that moment when we all lift our eyes and together take a breath.

Light in All Directions
Brandon Cesmat

Light in All Directions

I felt your gaze all day as you drove the road toward me.
That night in the observatory, we leaned into the telescope,
held our breath to focus on Jupiter with five moons
each lit like half-closed blind eyes,
all that old light taking eight minutes to reach us on
a planet close enough to catch light from a star.

Then you found Saturn, made out the rings standing on knife-point
and the band of shadow,
the dark older than the light,
the same dark just beyond the porch lamp,
the same constant dark between any two people.

A star sends its light in all directions
like a king dispatching navies that sink in the crossing except
one ship that arrives as you have
to make new whatever light survives.
Under that dome, dark so people could see stars,
I leaned against the wall and only your light fell onto me.

Pine Speak

I stand here by the grace of my scars.
On my trunk's downhill-side, see the burl
where wood isolated an infection, now like an eye's pupil.
All I have to say is, 'see?'
So, see the trunk's vertical line broken by my boughs.

I am implicated by gravity's law:
the dead bird beneath my limbs and
the needles I've dropped over him.
I'd do as much for you.

How well did I remember that bird?
Not well, they all move so fast.
My male and female pinecones together on the ground,
sex, sex, sex everywhere.
In all this death & duplication,
where is the love in this law?

Still, I claim innocence. Indifference is one of my gifts.
I am in the business of enfolding light,
absorbing water and minerals,
releasing my all as seeds.
I'm not proud of my scars.
My wood can rot or burn for all I care.

I tell you we are both blessed
to have made it this far
with anything to lose.

New poems by Brandon Cesmat

Howl, Hoot and Poem Disguised
for Leonidas

1 a.m. and I can't sleep like the owl
in the pine outside the front door.
He hoots a five-beat song with three notes.
and then rests while a car passes over the hill.

A coyote above the hum of
the air compressor on the casino roof.
He cries again at the top of the canyon.
I harmonize an inversion;
owl adds his refrain.

All of us nightsinging out,
then breathing in and listening.
What have we rustled out of cover?
I'm hungry for sleep but too tired
to tear the night apart and swallow it
as the dawn will.
At noon the canyon caves hold night's tongue.
Singing is the sound of hunger.
It's what we do with empty mouths.
It's what we live on when silence is not enough.

Queen Calafia at Home

O Queen Calafia,
have I told you lately how much I love you?
Mother you are,
receiving my feet first in Escondido,
where you hid me.

My Amazonian mama,
you need both mounts Whitney & Shasta,
Californios need all the snowy nipples we can get:
San Gorgonio, Palomar, San Jacinto.
You do not throw-down against Mexico.
Instead, you dangle Baja seductively south,
dip your toes in Cabo San Lucas.
I love how you rust away The Fence at Playas,
let it slip off like a bride at the reception slides a garter down,
remove it real slow, O Queen Calafia,
you know exactly what you're doing.

The wild horses on your mind in the Siskiyous
drag me over the Sierras where you embrace Nevada,
drag me onto the warm lap of your Mojave.
South of The Klamath, west of snowpack & Río Colorado,
east of The Pacific, you island us.

Your rivers and coast put fish on mariners' lines.
Your San Joaquin fills the farm laborer's hands.
Our municipalities choke your rivers while
tides slap away bluffs. Your coastline slips inland.
Queen Calafia, you're getting skinny.

Film noir flirts your wet-night boulevards,
multiplying streetlights beneath the hiring crimes.

How could our ancestors ever "settle" you?
Grid you, we try,
pitch the word *illegal as if it were a name, not*
a rock in a house of mirrors.
The glass twinkling down are not tears,
just a proliferation of mess to clean,
and whom will we hire to sweep?

O my queen, did I say how sorry we are?
We replace your endangered & extinct with peacocks and lapdogs.
LCDs and marquis in our eyes—not your stars,
especially not your sun: the way you gaze at it makes us golden.

How hard we work to ignore you.
From silted rivers to paved miracle smiles,
from the graves beneath the speed bumps,
we say to you iPad, iPhone, iPod but
I-I-I need to sing "God Save Queen California,"
un-Cupertino me from my cooped-up trance dance around the cul-du-sac.
I'm tired.
The beat has beaten my heart to death.
I have smog for breath.
I feel the crime of reloading without quoting,
as press-release crimes border my beliefs.

From depths of our deadbeat hearts, we say we love you,
while you shake. We've been dreaming you, but now I'm awake.
My thoughts return to you (my roots have never pulled away),
unaware yes, mind-full of the minuscule short money,
in obvious delusion oblivious to long-term remediation,
but Queen Calafia, don't say I'm losing you. I'm home. I'm home.
You are on my breath, the reason my words are moist.
Dehydrate me, ignite me, my queen. Make me *is here at home not seems.*

Mindscape Unlocked?
A Book of Poetry by Adam Funk

Apeirophobia

If death is what you fear,
Close your eyes and breathe.
Stillness overwhelms, and pain dissipates
From the pores of your skin—
Leaving you awash in the energy of your soul.

If love is what you fear,
Keep your eyes open, and look where you dive.
Inside the pools of blue, brown, or green
Lie the questions of every heart,
And the answers of every soul.

It consumes us all,
The fear of forever.
To confront it brings a nonexistent
Death to something that is incapable
Of decay.

Life

Life is poetry, regardless of form.
Forget the restrictions they put on expression.
Discussions start where writing ends,
And begins again on ellipsis

As if on an afterthought.
If Jim Carrey had met Plato,
Nietzsche would have been a comic.

Life would begin anew,
As if an ending…was an afterthought.

Poor EGO!
Plato would have become Freud's favorite patient if
He couldn't ramble on, destroying his teacher's mind.
He'd be rocking under a tree in a straightjacket, humming
"Allergies;"
And life would begin anew,
As if an ending…was an afterthought.
New stories beheld in Alexandria.
Dark ages would not exist.
Because Life would begin….afterthought…

Scene Rhapsodic

Swimming clouds of soft vermillion
Across inky skies bring the sharpest
Of contrasts to your oceanic eyes.

"Come home!" wails the wind,
Caressing the roots of your hair.
"Return to him" surfs the waves,
Crying tears you never knew were there.

He weeps, he cries, and waits for you
Upon the canvas of the night.
A beautiful meadow beside a dome house,
Built just perfect…just right.

A canvas that was painted upon, by long talks
Into the darkness, cradled by each other's minds.
Talks that you wish your body could sense
Through chains of technical confines.

You pointed out stars, and upon gravities drew
Your auras of every shade.
Laughing and joking, yet not hiding the beauty
Of all the plans you'd have to had made.

Do not leave the night unpainted,
Upon your easel wooden.
Paint by moonlight rimmed in orange…
To the sounds of sand held in hourglasses.

Create an artist's rhapsody to a writer's song!
If you write the music for me, I'll try to sing along.
And if you write the words to stories that shall remain unread.
I will put the ink to memory, every dash and dot into my head!

I write these words to waterfalls
As they jump into a brook.
I write a scene so wonderfully rhapsodic,
For your Forever Book.

In hopes that my call to the falcons
Will ride upon the sky!
To bring you back to me, unfettered,
So you can teach me how to fly!

Untitled
poems by Richard Kovac

To The Reader / A Modest Disclaimer

This book is me.
Maybe it will run
around the block
and meet several
of you.
That will be fine
(and fun for
fifteen dollars).
But please let me
go home again,
to do other chores
or just snore,
before it gets dark,
and feeble faults
are found; because
they are bound
to turn up. And it'll
cost me a scolding.

The Banner of the Last Hippie

The sign grew heavier
as he marched along
carrying its message
to culture and counterculture.
It said
"Make love not war!"
And what's more
he had been carrying it
in the great march
for forty lean and fat years.
His hands began to tremble
from Parkinson's,
but he continued to unfurl
his lonely banner,
as the crowd that had been
marching with him dissipated.
Finally he was the last witness
to hippiedom on earth.
"Make love not war!"
his feeble witness
to once hoped-for rebirth.

Wheels within Wheels
by Richard Kovac

Taken for Granted

Why are you moping today?
You wonder why no ones acknowledges you.
The answer is simple,
you are too graceful and lovely for us.
We can't praise you, or even, sometimes,
notice that you are here.
No more do fish acknowledge water.
You stay as invisible as light
thru the window with your flower pots.
No, when all is well, we don't note
your ironing, driving, cooked meals,
fresh smelling laundry, smiles,
clean towels, or the usual glad hug;
and your sprightly conversation is
also taken for granted.
Maybe if you tripped and screamed.
Maybe if you tried to poison us.
Then we'd notice.

You're a happy element of the universe
we're in willy-nilly.
Isn't that praise?
Then how come you're moping today?
Are you all right?
But Elizabeth didn't answer, and
spent two days in bed.
The flowers got brown, and
the goldfish dropped dead.

Obit for the Twin Towers

A lesson of 9/11
is not to assault heaven.
It is necessary to keep
a low profile
to survive.
It is arrogant to assault
heaven, as the World Trade Center
and myself
have done.
Therefore I have not thrived.

The towers were emblems
of wealth and power,
but the victims were mere humans.
I grieve for them, and me.
We come from the same country,
which I have sometimes
treated as if it were Babylon
but like to gaze upon.

To disarm these enemies
who fanatically hate us,
love them; and explore
whence their grudges stem.
But again I'm not keeping
a low profile.
It's OK to smile
at my conceit
in this inadequate obit
for the Twin Towers
of Manhattan,
and me.
I had been there many times.

The Benign Tree
poetry by Richard Kovac

Laboring Forth

Part I
If giving birth is labor,
then all labor is giving birth.
The working class produces
the material fabric
of the universe,
from steel bolts
to stainless laser beams,
but the looms of the universe
must be unionized,
if the inhabitants
are to smile at what
has been created.
What labor gives birth to
is humanity.

Part II
He worked hard
but a house and four children
were supported by the union.
These were the good old days.
It was CWA
and I belonged to AFSCME.
We were grateful
after a fashion.
"The union got us
all we got," said someone.
Those days are gone.
The minimum wage hardly
supports a family of one.

Only we have more gewgaws
and gimmickry and gadgets —
But what have we won?
It's time for the unions
to wake up again.
Why have the unions been asleep?
Service industries await them,
and so do sweatshops in Indonesia.

Keats' Hoax

This hoax
supports,
surmises
beyond grasp,
otherwise,
like the truth
of the thorned rose
and the pond lotus,
it makes me think
that it is not,
then, a hoax,
and beauty
really is

Timewinds
poems by Lee Underwood

I don't know much about God,
But I do know

She's black, with blue eyes,
      Speaks Hebrew, and loves French pastry.
      When she turns around,
He's a red-headed, brown-eyed Swede who
      Speaks Tibetan with a Peruvian accent.
      When he looks to the left,
She's Asian-yellow, 5'9" tall,
      And her Icelandic chitchat sounds like Italian.
      When she looks to the right,
He's a green-eyed Indian Sikh who
      Writes Spanish, and sells real estate in Brooklyn.
      When he backflips,
She's a gentle orangutan from Borneo,
      With hazel eyes, flowers in her hair,
      Thunderclouds and warm rainshowers in her hands.
      When she swings on vines,
He's an Arctic polar bear, with blue sky in his eyes,
      And all the world's oceans whispering in his ears.
      When he playfully slides down a snow-slope,
She's a two-year-old little girl,
      With blonde and red and black hair,
      Who counts to three in 500 languages,
      And cries and laughs in one language that
      Mothers all over the world understand.

So what's to know?
      Here, have a strawberry dipped in powdered sugar.
      God is also delicious!

For Tim Buckley

There were seawaves then, my friend,
Moonlight glittering among
Spikey shadowed palm leaves
Spread like veils 'cross
Luminescent Venice summer beaches,
Sea-salt in balmy night air,
Midnight ocean waters
Brushing close,
Whispering our youth to us,
Gentle kisses lapping sand-swaths,
Cream-foam licking shoreline edges —

Time passed inside an hour glass,
Stared up at stars,
And laughed.

Now, again —
After more than 40 years,
Finally recognized, appreciated, celebrated,
Given your proper respect —
You speak to me from far across these waters,
Your voice alluring, entrancing, seductive,
Your gentle windsong
Whisper-intimate,
Brimming with tears,
With yearning's aching arc,
Compassion's understanding,
Jingling silver in moonlight,
Bitterly sweet in

Empathy, hope, heartbreak,
Happy/sad again,
And here you are,
Calling from afar —
And I hear you.

How the music
In our life and love
Made all the difference.
We were exactly
What we needed
At the time.
Few have known
A melody like ours,
And, yes,
I hear you calling.

Soon enough,
I softly cry,
Soon enough
I will join you, yes,
When the hourglass tilts,
And laughs again.

TRIAL AND ERROR: The Education of a Freedom Lawyer—
Volume One: For the Defense; Volume Two: For the
Prosecution; Volume Three: Return to the Defense
by law professor Arthur W. Campbell

Introduction (excerpt Volume III)

Who and what are freedom lawyers? They come in every size, age, and gender. They practice in all fields of law. They work in every section of the globe and quarter of society. They aim to foster human freedom and oppose injustice.

Two prior volumes in this trilogy depicted me in roles most people see as polar opposites: first, criminal defense attorney and then as prosecutor. In each role I pulled a different end of rope our adversary system uses in its tug-of-war. Yet that rope of justice stayed the same.

Each episode revealed different challenges as I confronted forces, both external and internal, that stood between my clients and my view of justice in their case.

My first book's trials introduced me to the depth and breadth of justice in a court of law— surprises, flukes, and defects intermixed with pragmatism, truth, and politics.

The second volume recognized a potent comrade in the courtroom. Beside my freedom lawyer stalked a warrior who would fight for victory at all costs. Once those costs meant I convicted someone who was innocent— and the price I paid to set him free.

Not until the middle of the current volume did I discover what my warrior fed upon. That resolved much turmoil in my life— as a lawyer and a man— and led to probing deeper towards my core.

Blowing dust from private trial notes helped me draft the first two books. But when I reached this volume's murder case I'd ceased keeping notes. Nonetheless some clients of that time still stamp down hallways of my mind; now they mingle in a single chapter: "Further Freedom-Law Adventures.

As before, and out of similar regard for peoples' privacy, these pages often cloak their characters with pseudonyms and fictionalized peripherals.

This book brings readers through my final years in Washington, D.C., touches on my life in academia, and concludes with People versus Drusilla Campbell et alia.
At that time it was the largest mass-protest trial in San Diego history. It was the last and most important trial of my career. Yes, the lead defendant was my wife.

* * * * *

Excepts Volume III

Further Freedom-Law Adventures

No man is above the law— and no man below it.
— Theodore Roosevelt

Years before I earned my law degrees, I dreamt someday I'd be a sole practitioner in San Francisco. My full-color vision involved offices with Berber rugs and walnut walls. While still in the District of Columbia some non-trial clients fueled this fantasy. They're depicted here.

* * * * *

Throughout this trilogy I've mentioned lessons learned from Thomas L. ("Cut") Cummings, my favorite client in book one. The following incident occurred not long before he died.
At home one sizzling summer eve in Virginia's countryside, Dru and I were set to make the 30-minute drive to D.C. and a party with some friends. I snatched our jingling kitchen phone. The deep voice inside was unmistakable: Cut.

"I'm sorry to bother you, Mr. Campbell, but 4th precinct cops just busted me for ADW [assault with a deadly weapon.] Some guy jumped me in an alley, so I opened up a can of whoop-ass and karate-kicked him to the ground. But cops checked my record and decided they would call my shoe a 'deadly weapon.' Can you come down and stand my bail?"

"No problem, Cut. Dru and I will be there in an hour." When we arrived I related my intention to a frazzled duty sergeant. Too busy to attend me, he pointed to a bench along the wall. Dru and I sat down beside a dozen other citizens with Friday-night demands.

Fifteen minutes later an assistant sauntered to our spot. Looking at Dru's au courant snug blouse and leather miniskirt, he asked, "What happened, baby— someone knock you up?" I looked away and tried to stifle my guffaws. Outraged at the time, Dru now laughingly recounts his jive.

* * * * *

Excepts Volume III

Next spring freedom lawyer felt another surge. The American Civil Liberties Union asked if I would represent four women housed in Lorton Prison on the outskirts of D.C. They were charged with seizing one wing of the penal complex, as part of an attempted inmate takeover of the facility.

The U.S. Attorney's office had subpoenaed them to testify about the episode before a grand jury. I learned five other inmates had spearheaded the revolt; they were the bulls-eye on the prosecutor's target. But my clients risked extended prison terms if they refused to talk about the incident.

After checking out the facts and law, I spent half-a-dozen hours parleying with prosecutors. I was able to secure complete immunity for my four clients. In exchange for truthful testimony, they'd be safe from any charges that arose from their part in the mutiny.

This little triumph triggered a surprising second victory. My clients' evidence disclosed what lay beneath the insurrection— many disregarded long-term, inmategrievances. So, despite insistence by the prosecutor, the
grand jury wouldn't bring indictments against any prisoner in the protest takeover.

Reflecting on these episodes, I realized my scope of freedom law had grown beyond encounters in a courtroom. I'd learned to penetrate the courthouse smoke and mirrors. Now I could negotiate with folks who jiggered levers of the law inside the wizard's lair.

The Postman
by Mun Duk-su

from the Forward by Yearn Hong Choi

As I come to read Mun Dok-su's long poem, "The Postman" I am pleased to know that one of Korea's most revered poets is still doing productive writing. I admire his work.

. . .

Mun was drafted early in the Korean War (1950-53), and was commissioned as an army lieutenant. He was wounded in the front line, at the location referred to as the Iron Triangle. Because of his injury, he retired from active duty. His war experiences influenced his work as a humanitarian poet and writer.

(Mun Suk-su's poem , The Postman, was written out of his Korean War experience. In 2010 Mun was nominate for the Nobel Prize in Literture. Poetic Matrix Press' volume of The Postman was part of his presentation to the Nobel Committee.)

from The Postman

4. DMZ
In the satchel, dancing on gaunt haunches, jerking,
is a rifle broken in two like a stick.
Iron bridges spanning the Yalu[20] and Imjin[21] rivers are mere toys.
The caterpillar tracks of the Soviet-made T34s
that startled the South that Sunday morning
are nothing but paper, all crushed flat.
There are many farewell messages, once tied round necks, fallen,
the writers invisible now:
where have all the addressees gone?

Wearing helmets and long black boots
from the mouth of the Imjin River via Kimhwa and Ch'ŏlwon
   toward Kosŏng

following the ups and downs of latitude is of no small importance.
They swagger along as though it all belongs to them.
Leaving behind the line where they confronted one another, guns aimed,
South and North are each obliged to pull back two kilometers.
Kindly hands drive in iron posts at regular intervals,
drive them in with weighty hammers.
They sink deep into earth soft as tender flesh. It hurts.
Wearing helmets got from somewhere, they erect and unroll fences
  of barbed wire
stretching 155 miles from west to east without a break.

So land and nation are divided in two,
divided at the waist, families separated, severed,
a vortex of pain, grief, bitterness, tears
that like clouds and winds and sky know nothing of North and South.
Cranes lay eggs in nests on high pine-tree branches,
squirrels, boars, hares frolic and play,
in green groves the pale bodies of deer gleam occasionally,
this DMZ inside its tangles of barbed wire.

>   As if the void has finished reading a generation's depths
>   it bounces off with a *bang*.
>   Like a ping-pong ball slowly swelling like a balloon, it rolls away.
>   At a kick from soccer players' feet it goes to Manchester,
>   Milan, and back.
>
>   You can't stay put quietly in one place, can you?
>   You want to orbit the whole world once you're struck
>   by the bat.
>   The brand of void in that bulging postman's satchel
>   you're bearing
>   is the zero Indians were the first to discover, isn't it?
>   If you pierce the deep walls of geological strata

From that gap emerges like a stream of urine a sound of pure water
whose source is far away;
playing spoilt and humming like children,
it wakes the weary sleeper.

      The ball of the void is rolling off.
      But it's not rolling off like a skull. In the desert and in the ocean
      rolling, rolling, trundling, trundling, tumbling, tumbling, revolving on
      delving deep into the desert, roundly rolling,
      rolls down into the sea, several lengths of silk unfurling.
      Wind, gas, starvation, despair, shellfire, nuclear mushroom cloud,
      forcing your way inside, grinding, reducing to powder,
      you go rolling on.

Your lungs were blocked by Australian sandstorms,
then in 2004 or so, wandering lost in the groves of Mediterranean myth,
you tasted the enticing apple
that boastful Paris awarded to Miss Aphrodite.

      Sharing that apple with your wife
      you munched the depths of a myth ripened in the hue
      of the Mediterranean.
      And briefly you glimpsed Themis, a sharp sword in her
      left hand,
      her eyes blindfolded, holding a set of scales in her right hand.

Raising up rocks toppled by earthquakes,
pulling apart the gaps in broken bricks and penetrating like a ray of light,
you bounced off gaping windpipes
but even in Sumatra's Aceh and in Sichuan

      the ball hit the floor and rebounded.
      It went higher than you, higher than Mount Pukhan.

> After turning once round the pure water at Mount Paekdu's 2,700 meters
> rolling across the Sea of Galilee on which Jesus walked bare-footed
> at the peak of Everest's 8,848 meters
> as well as that rock seen in Lumbini on which Siddhartha's gaze lingered

The ball erases itself.
As it rolls on it erases its own every gesture.
Flying on, it erases the path it has taken.
Even in the midst of explosions and slaughter,
breathing, it erases.
It even erases the way it erases.
The interior, exterior of the office
and all that surges to fill the city's labyrinth,
cannot be touched or seen, yet
rising, as if cultivating trees or flowers,
300 stories to the 300th story, all erased,
even my army registration number 213360.
Figure by figure the number of beading drops of blood
flies away like birds lined up on an electric wire.

Render
by Joseph Zaccardi

There is a River

There is a river near Hue called Perfume;
its water is red, amber during the monsoons.
There is a factory that processes rubber,
trees with thick green leaves, barks bleeding white.
Birds come from around the world to drink
from the river. I used to watch them hop, dip
their heads, then leap up into air, folding
their legs back like a jet's wheels, like Corsairs.
And there is someone named Du Thanh Mai
who once took me into her house, fed me
rice with her fingers, while I tilted my head
back and chewed. She showed me her white
jade Buddhas. And said, I should listen
to the stars out in her small garden because
they could sing. There was a cot to lie upon,
around us bamboo and boxes of lilies, some burnt
orange, some white, some darker. And one
that was green with white pistils.
There was fragrance and river sound. I know
we both cried, and if either of us slept,
it was pretend.

Walking in the Woods Toward Jade Mountain

In the green world there are green birds,
and they hop on the tops of lichee trees
and eat the sweet flesh. You would not know
they were there except for their singing,
but if your ears are stuffed full with your
own thoughts or the music of daydreaming,
they will pepper you with seeds and shake
the green light with their green feathers.
They will perch on branches of green willow,
talk in their green language until you listen.
They know all the stories in every tongue
by heart, and know each word is a gift
having more than one meaning. They know
the Chinese sound for ten thousand
was once the same as the sound for scorpion.
To the green birds, there is no difference.

New poems by Joseph Zaccardi

Black Sand River

Peach petals drift downstream from a hidden world at peace;
Green birds feed among green rushes of the middle reaches.

Last year there was spring and this year spring;
Last year the mountain streams were still.

Last year the loquat blossoms shriveled.
Now the rains have returned.

In the woods the sound of trees falling.
Ten thousand trees surround one tree.

A brother and sister have drowned.
The nature of water is to be water.

Green birds in the floodplains;
Trees of jade and trees of pearl.

The rushes retreat and surge.
Who wants to be alone?

Celestial Stems, Earthly Branches

If I could live in the woods among ferns and old pines,
I would fill a room with blue mountains.

In both places would be a fire and a flagon of wine,
And the days would breathe at either end and disappear.

What ceases to be is as natural as what comes to be:
Dried tea leaves release their fragrance to boiling water.

In sleep, the mind scatters briar and blackberry seeds.
Sows weeds and bean vines
                              sows reeds and tares.

Whimsy, Reticence & Laud unuly sonnets
by Grace Marie Grafton

Evoke

The arabesque melody. I want. Song
of the frog, song of the blue damselfly
to placate the welts rising inconsolably
on my classical score. It's too wary,
too fretful. It wears a straight mouth, it wears
tight hose. More nakedness please, more slippage.
The raucous raven's song, boisterous,
irreverent. Oh blaring trumpet, tickling
timpani, but I don't stop there. Open
the back door, open sequestered dawns,
midnight rain, the small silver fish.
I sit on the limb, lean against the trunk,
ask permission of the doves to watch them
set on eggs and create grey, create brown.

Revelation

Break apart. Break sky, break earth, break bone.
It's past choice, past escape – indoors or
cloistered in armor. Stand up straight or bend
under the force of light. Rain and clouds' shift
and all I thought I was – feathers in the
wind. No longer a garden, no more
a musical note. Mud is slippery.
There's a great laughing in the arc.
I wouldn't call it hope and it can't be caught.
But those feathers that were yanked from my
shoulders are arrayed now in late sunlight,
the crack in the sky widened to pour to earth
a sticky something that anchors feet.
I have no more need to fly.

— NON-FICTION —

Composing Temple Sunrise:
Overcoming Writer's Block at Burning Man
By Hassan El-Tayyab

Composing Temple Sunrise is a memoir odyssey: crossing the country; meeting Fishbug; going to Burning Man; writing music; with side stories on being Bedoiun in the US.

from Chapter 26

"Travel is fatal to prejudice, bigotry, and narrow-mindedness."
— Mark Twain

After Fishbug's dawn show I glanced across the Playa and felt a pang of sadness. Later that evening a spark at the base of The Man would turn into a massive fire and turn the wood structure into hot coals and ash. The festival's centerpiece would be gone and the last two days of Burning Man would blow by like a gust of playa wind.

A short walk across the Playa brought me to a tent called Muhammad's right off the Esplanade. The structure was about twenty feet across and ten feet to the back wall. The brown fabric was supported by thick wooden beams and staked with ropes. An ankle high coffee table covered in a blue and white star patterned tablecloth stretched the tent's entire length. Costumed Burners lounged on plush multicolored cushions and blankets, sipping mixed drinks in martini glasses. In the center was a gold and blue hookah with three checkered hoses and a bright glowing coal at the top. Smoke wafted upward and collected near the ceiling.

"Care for a Margarita?" inquired the host.

The vibe at Muhammad's was relaxed. I sat back and took occasional puffs on a hookah while sipping from the constant flow of mixed drinks coming my way. Every time my glass got down to half full it was filled up again. The experience reminded me of my family in Jordan and the summer I finally went to go visit them. The generosity. The dust. The place of my dad's birth. I let my mind drift.

I had been to Jordan once before when I was five but had little recollection of the trip. All I remember was a smelly camel ride and sitting on a lush carpet at my grandparents house eating Cheerios. Mom told me some stories that involved a family feud she witnessed resolved by two community elders dressed in cloaks wearing jeweled daggers at their hips. The rest of my memories are in the form of pictures in Dad's photo albums. Pictures of my grandmother wearing tribal paint on her face and my grandfather wearing traditional Bedouin garb. I always wished I had gotten to know them before they passed away.

Dad had been trying to get me to come visit Jordan for a long time and the timing finally worked out in August of 2007. I had close friends ask me why I wanted to go considering my strained relationship with my father. I'd tell them that no matter what had happened with Dad and Mom, I deserved to see where I came from.

My flight on Royal Jordanian Airlines took about 17 hours. I remember looking out at the glowing sunset over the Atlantic Ocean dreaming of Jordan. Dreaming of seeing my dad again.

My father and two uncles picked me up from the airport terminal in Amman.

"As-salam alaykum." Dad glowed when he saw his eldest son and gave me wet kisses on both cheeks and a long suffocating hug. He had greyed significantly since the last time I had seen him. He was an old man now.

"Alaykum salam." I said back wiping the saliva from my cheek with mixed emotions.

The rest of the drive to Madaba was narrated in Arabic. We drove nineteen miles south through the center of Jordan winding through tightly packed thoroughfares, traffic cirles, and erratic driving. From the car window I saw a man burning trash on the side of the road filling the air with a putrid smell. Behind the man stood a giant billboard paid for by the royal family. It said in both Arabic and English: *We look to a brighter future.*

We pulled up a side street and I deduced that we had arrived home. I saw no signs to indicate where we were though. It's not unordinary for streets in Jordan to be nameless. On this particular unnamed street, all five houses were owned exclusively by El-Tayyabs. To me it was El-Tayyab St. My aunt and uncles each owned a house on the street and lived there with their children and grandchildren. It was a multi-generational extended family living on the same unnamed road under adjacent roofs.

In the first house on El-Tayyab St. lived my dad's sister Roia and her kids Muhammad, Facep, Ahmed, and Hamnah. Next to Dad's house lived my uncle Hallad with his wife Selema and their six kids Faris, Feraz, Bedir, Abir, Adra, and Fahad. They also have six grand children. Next to Hallad lived my eldest Uncle Omar, his wife Fatima, and their eight children and three grand children Muhammad, Abdoula, Ahmed, Alia, Alla, Ruba, Ali, Naof, Sharif, Fatima, and Omar. The last house on the block is my dad's uncle Issa's home where he and his four children Muhammad, Ahmed, Isha, and Couter live.

I got out of the car with my luggage surrounded by family. *My family.* My long lost Bedouin tribe. Children ran around me and shrieked with laughter at me as they chased each other. With a hug and a kiss on either cheek my relatives embraced me, a family member they had missed for two decades. A family I had missed too.

Like Fallen Snow
Memoir with Poetry Ruth Rosenthal

In the Midst of Plenty

We walked past the many booths of food, brilliant glazed ceramics, artwork of every kind, bright colorful clothing and live music every few feet. When we heard jazz we looked for seats. A friend was there. After warm greetings he brought three chairs together so we could listen in comfort.

The weather was just what people want for an outdoor arts and crafts festival, hot, but not too hot. There wasn't a strong breeze, just enough to keep from feeling too warm.

We spoke, catching up with ourselves since we'd last met. But mostly we listened to the good music we'd come to hear. His cousin plays piano. He's had a long-standing gig in San Francisco. There was a man on acoustic bass who'd had the same city gig with him for many years. The club owner dropped his costs and let him go. Just like the affluent town this festival was in: the same bass player —a fine musician—but that has nothing to do with it, was hired for part of the day. The cousin would have to solo the rest of the afternoon.

The bass player packed up and left. The piano player took a break. He stood, talking with someone, in front of the heavy wood lattice backdrop. The street, blocked off, had a green plastic covering where the musicians had set up.

Before anyone could react the tall weighty backdrop toppled, barely missing the piano player.

For a moment everything stopped in that little corner of the street fair. Nobody moved. Then people went back to their eating and conversation as though nothing had happened.

Colors swirled in the light breeze: multi-colored table umbrellas, rainbows of clothing, plates of ethnic Picasso-like varieties and colorful speech seemed to blend in the bright afternoon.

Out of a corner of the eye appeared a nebech. A nebech is a being for whom others feel anything from pity to contempt. He wore a wide brimmed dirty hat. His beard was long and thick and needed to be washed like all the rest of him. His huge winter coat had a zigzag tear big enough for him to put both feet through together. He looked like he had stepped out of a black and white movie into a technicolor world.

Without a word he reached to help the piano player lift the fallen backdrop. They set it on its side where it could do no damage.

That done, he walked back to the grocery cart that held his few possessions and left the festive scene.

In the Garden of Life

Stay in the garden of Life
where your own thoughts
embrace you
with the light
of your own making.

Stay and listen to the quiet
of your own being.
Still yourself
to hear the color
of your blossoms
that are the music
of your life.

Song of Myself: A Korean-American Life
A Memoir By Yearn Hong Choi

Introduction

The Orientals were inscrutable! They are still inscrutable. I want to present my "inscrutable" life to America with this book. This is a song of myself. This is my life as a Korean-American from the first moment I landed in Seattle on May 30, 1968, to today.

When I look back on my life in America, I think first of the great events I was witness to. I particularly think of the political protest movements, which I believe show the greatness of America. The years of protest against the Vietnam War, the civil rights movement and the rise environmental protection — each in its own way showed the strength and openness of this new country. A turbulent era put the United States' creative minds and energy on full display. Lately, I have experienced a kind of déjà vu watching Barack Obama's candidacy and victory in the 2008 presidential election. It is an exhilarating time all over again. Can America return itself to true greatness?

When I look back on my life here, I also think of the personal honors I had as a scholar, a poet, a government official and a political writer. Each, it seems, was tempered by an unexpected personal trial. I came to this country with a few hundred dollars and ended up a college professor — a great honor. But my tenure evaluation at one university offered the first real sadness in my life, when I was denied tenure. I was a victim of racial discrimination, I concluded — I was denied even though my qualifications were equal to or better than those of my peers. There was ample evidence that the school disliked the "overrepresentation" of foreign faculty. And so they denied me. Others, wrongly I thought, claimed it was "my accent." This was the first time I ever saw my own limitations. I came to know them, and confront them with humility — a growing experience. Around the same time I was happy to become father of two children and to watch one become a fine young man and the other a fine young woman — an even greater growing experience.

I also think of my honors. One was becoming a high-level government bureaucrat-scholar in the Office of the Secretary of Defense. Imagine that — a foreign-born naturalized citizen who gets to work for the Secretary of Defense! My position was assistant for environmental quality. In that position, I also felt frustration, though of a different sort. I expended much energy, and looked with much hope, on the subject of radioactive waste management. I believed in the capacity of this country to solve pressing environmental problems surrounding such dangerous materials. But the 1980 and 1982 radioactive waste management acts the U.S. Congress passed have not made much progress even today, after more than 20 years. This showed me that America has its own limits. We need nuclear energy, nuclear research and nuclear medicine, but we don't care much about properly handling the waste generated from nuclear activities. Every time, the vagaries of the federal system conspire to stop reasonable agreements. My own view is that nuclear arms should be banned — but the waste from producing the existing nuclear weapons can and should be safely disposed of for good, since the activities that produce it are so vital. It never happens.

A Korean-American Life in Washington/Literary Activities

Gwendolyn Brooks and Reed Whittemore

In the 1980s I met Edward Reed Whittemore, Poet Laureate of Maryland, while teaching at the University of Maryland. I also met Gwendolyn Brooks, the Pulitzer Prize-winning poet. Those who know poetry will know Whittemore and most educated Americans will recognize Brooks, a famous poet and poetess. Both poets served as Library of Congress Poetry Consultants. Later the title of "Poetry Consultant" was changed to the more prestigious-sounding "Poet Laureate."

When my first poetry book in English, *Autumn Vocabularies*, was published by the Writers' Workshop in Calcutta, India, Gwendolyn Brooks sent me a poem, "Yearn Hong Choi." I used it in my poetry book. She encouraged and cheered me to continue my poetry writing. I miss her.

Yearn Hong Choi poem

Here is a man consciously in the world.
He looks, he sees, he executes, he deplores.
He capsulizes! He magnifies!
He knows that one of the ingredients of human
Existence is infamy, that another is cold cruelty,
That another is weakness.
But he is also aware of positives — and of nuances
That whisper of potential.
He is a skillful wielder of language.
He uses language with sensitive enjoyment, with
Canny respect.
Yearn Hong Choi is a new influencer and enhancer.
        Gwendolyn Brooks

Second Poetry Reading in the Library of Congress
Yearn Hong Choi

In January 2003, I was invited to read my poems at the Library of Congress a second time, this time on the celebration occasion of the centennial year of Koreas' laborers' landing in the Hawaii sugar plantations in the early 20th century. In the same year, I edited *Surfacing Sadness: A Centennial of Korean-American Literature* (Homa and Sekey Books). Here are some of the poems I read, many reflecting on my American life.

Black Korean

The Korea man moved to Hawaiian sugar plantation
At the turn of the century,
and then to Mexico's henequen field,
and finally moved to Cuba's sugar plantation
to make a few dollars.
His grandson, I met in the District of Columbia,
only knew that his grandpa was a Korea man,
but did not know why he was in Cuba.
The old man was supposedly in the hermit kingdom.
The Korea man fell in love with a black woman in Cuba,
And had a son, and his son moved to Miami as a refugee,
then to the District of Columbia.
Jose Suh, I know, has an odd last name.
The Chosun's seed was not just planted in Cuba.
It was also planted in the Central Asia desert,
and the cold wind of Sakhalin
as well.
I see a Korea man's anger, frustration, love
and affection in the black of his grandson.
I see the demise of the Chosun kingdom in a Black-Korean-American from Cuba,
and the Korean's odyssey.

Reminiscence

A certain coquettish Korean girl
Is my only memory of my Indiana University.
Oh, how flirtatious she was!
I cannot even begin.
She sang always, dreaming of
Being an opera singer someday.
I applauded her dream.
By time and tide
I am older and wiser since my university days.
Even if I see her now
I doubt I would blush as I used to so often then.
My heart yearns for those carefree days—
The innocent days of my youth so long ago—
Wishing to become as a young man once again.
The beautiful campus is still vivid in my memory.
I wonder if the splendor of the green field
Is still the same.
Music by Bach that she and I used to appreciate
May still permeate the fresh air on campus.
There was a beautiful prelude of a young couple.
There was nothing but an overture of young lovers' opera.

Triumph at Last: A Korean-American Life
A Memoir by Steven Soo Hyun Kim

Introduction (excerpts)

Life is a journey. Having grown up in a poor mountain village in Korea, I can think of only one word that describes my youth: destitute. Korea was a very poor nation, my family barely scraped by. Hunger and starvation were my life. Malnutrition was a luxury.

I worked as a "farm boy" and begged food from the neighbors. At fourteen, I went to the city of Pohang alone to get my education. In Pohang I earned a meager income working during the day and studying at a middle school at night. I completed my high school in Taegu, capital of North Kyungsang Province.

For my military duty I was fortunately assigned to the Korean Army Headquarters in Seoul. I thought that this move to Seoul was a sign of a blessing from God. My soldier's life in Seoul offered me a chance to study at Sung Kyun Kwan University at night. As a soldier, I also witnessed General Park Chung-hee's Army coup d'etat during the morning of May 16, 1961 in the Korean Army Headquarters.

My insurmountable poverty once drove me to commit suicide in college. But I was fortunately unsuccessful. Since then, I have done my best to improve my fate everyday, while reciting, "Life is so beautiful!" I decided to study civil engineering at my second college, Chunggu University, later to become one big university outside the city of Taegu, – Youngnam University – after absorbing Taegu University as well.

. . . .

My memoir is of course a reflection of my personal life, but it is also a reflection of the times and places I have lived and worked. So this book is a composition of my experiences, starting in poverty-stricken Korea in the 40s and 50s, then during Korea's drive toward modernization, and then to my experience in the Vietnam War in the

1960s, and finally to my life in the United States of America as a civil engineer. I feel proud to have contributed to the city of Atlanta in my career as a civil engineer. My projects have included drafting and constructing Atlanta's waste water plant; constructing the 70-story Peachtree Plaza Hotel; and Georgia Tech's Urban Life Center and Gym.

    My memoir is also a reflection of my life as a Korean-American in the Atlanta community since I arrived in 1970. I have met many nice people in the course of my life and want to express my gratitude to them in this book. I owe a lot to them. Lastly, I am thankful to my wife Young-ja for her endless love and our children Carol, James, and Tracy and their wonderful growth into adulthood.

    I am grateful for what I have possessed — life, liberty and the pursuit of happiness. But I have never forgotten my early destitute life, so I have been more grateful to the Lord everyday. I will pursue my future with endless dreams and hopes.

    With this book, I hope that each reader can share in and experience my truly humble life story.

Steven Soo-Hyun Kim
Marietta, Georgia

. . . .

1
One Hungry Boy in the Flowering Mountain Village
—In Search of the Hometown

Hunger, Despair, and Funeral (excerpt)

One was different from the other: Living in Korea under the Japanese rule was one thing, and living in Japan as a Korean was another. The latter was sadder than the former. It was a tragedy for the Koreans living in Japan – who annexed Korea for 40 years as its colony.

Under the Japanese colonial rule, Korean people valued liberty and independence above all else. Therefore, my parents, actually just my father and grandpa, wanted nothing more than to move back to their homeland, giving up everything they achieved from their hard work during their 25 years in Japan and return to Korea when independence was achieved in August 1945. Japan was their country with sweat and tears for a relatively long time, but they made a decision to return to their home country.

I was born on November 28, 1936 in Tokyo, Japan as the second son, or third child of my father, Kim Sang-dong, and mother, Kim Soon-jo. My father was a member of the Andong Kim clan. He was proud of his family name and background. Many famous patriots and high-ranking government officials in the Chosun Kingdom were produced from his Kim clan. My parents told me that I was born in the year Mr. Sohn Ki-jung won the Berlin Olympics' marathon. Sohn was a Korean marathoner but ran under the Japanese flag because Korea had not had its sovereignty for 31 years. The Korean newspapers reported Sohn's victory, but hid the fact that he won a medal for the Japanese by erasing the Japanese flag on his uniform at the gold medal award ceremony. He was the first Korean winner in Olympic history.

When I was 8-years old, I entered elementary school at Haneda, Tokyo, but the Allied Forces raided the Tokyo area everyday and night, so that our family moved to a village named Kiso, Fukushima. There, I heard the surrender of the Japanese Emperor to the Commander of the Allied Forces. That was the moment of the Liberation of Korea from the Japanese yoke.

When I look back on my childhood, I realize that my life was not normal: I was born in a foreign country, lived through the War as a school child, and crossed the sea to return to my parents' home country at a tender age. My parents were so happy to hear the Japanese Emperor's surrender statement on August 15, 1945, but could not express their feeling in front of the Japanese people. Following the liberation, my father unquestionably pushed his desire to return to Korea, but my mother was more realistic about comparing and contrasting life in Japan and Korea. To her, her home was in Japan. Her life was there, not in Korea. She believed in the fact that no one was waiting for them in Korea and she knew a simple fact, that liberty in Japan would ease the hardship of feeding her family three meals a day. However, my father was adamant and he ultimately prevailed in the debate. My father's parents sided with him. My mother made good sense. Mother did not yield. She knew that going home would be a new tough beginning, worse than living in Kiso, Fukushima. Mother was alone and could not win the majority.

. . . .

NATURE JOURNAL WITH JOHN MUIR, A WRITING JOURNAL
Edited by Bonnie Joanna Gisel

Quotes by John Muir

> Come all who need rest and light bending and breaking with over work, leave your profits and losses and metallic dividends and come a beeing.

The grand, priest-like pines held their arms above us in blessing; the wind sang songs of welcome; the cool glaciers and the running crystal foundations added their greetings. I was no longer on, but in the mountains: home again, and my pulses were filled. On and on reveling in white moonlight spangles on the streams, shadows in rock hollows and briery ravines, tree architecture on the sky, more divine than ever stars in their spires, leafy mosaic on meadow and bank. Never had the Sierra seemed so inexhaustible. Mile on mile onward in the forest through groves old and young. Pine tassels overarched and brushed both cheeks at once. The chirping of crickets only deepened the stillness.

> The walker making the best excursion in pure wilderness. Not necessarily the longest and most dangerous excursion up the highest mountains, through the deepest woods or across the widest torrents, glaciers or deserts, but the one, however, short or long, rough or smooth, calm or stormy, on which the able, fearless walker sees most, learns most, loves most and leaves the cleanest track. Whose heart and mind grow naturally, like trees, gathering inspiration from everything....who learns to regard everything about him as friends and neighbors—the stars, the earth, planets and animals, as well as men.

— 187

Muir Ramble Route Walking from San Francisco to Yosemite In the Footsteps of John Muir
A Guide for hiking from San Francisco to Yosemite
by Peter and Donna Thomas

Introduction

In the early morning of March 28, 1868, twenty-nine year old John Muir stepped off the crowded steamship "Nebraska" into the busy San Francisco waterfront. He had just arrived from New York, via Panama, had been cooped up on the ship with a "barbarous mob" for much too long, and was ready to "get to the uncultivated wild part of the state." He asked the first person he encountered for directions and then set off on what would be a six week long, three hundred mile trip across California to Yosemite.

In 1868 John Muir was just another of the many thousands of hopeful immigrants and curious visitors who have arrived in California hoping to make their fortune or have the opportunity to see the natural wonders of the state. Today he is internationally recognized as a founder of the Sierra Club, the man who talked President Roosevelt into making Yosemite a National Park and a prominent figure in the development of the modern environmental and conservation movements. He is also the man on the California quarter and he is there for a good reason. Like Washington and Lincoln, he was a hero.

John Muir was an explorer, a feel-no-pain adventurer, a hardcore mountaineer, and a deeply religious man who ecstatically saw God in all nature. Today he is a role model for people who love nature and the outdoors. Anyone who has hiked in the Sierra has probably heard the story about how he would just grab a loaf of bread, put a few bags of tea in his pocket, throw a coat over his shoulder and head off into the Sierra. In this era of urban sprawl and mega-highways crisscrossing the landscape, it is an amazing, almost magical thing to ponder: that a person could walk across California to Yosemite.

Even in 1868, the year before the completion of the transcontinental railroad, Yosemite, with its immense granite cliffs, huge waterfalls and giant trees, was already a tourist destination. The first travel guide to Yosemite, "Scenes of Wonder and Curiosity in California" was published in 1862. In it the author, James M. Hutchings, describes Yosemite as a "wonder of the world", a place to see before you die. Hutchings even details the best route to get there from San Francisco, advising the reader to take the ferry to Stockton, a stage to Coulterville, and then enter the Yosemite Valley on horseback.

Muir did not follow Hutchings' advice. He walked. As Muir wrote: "…we had plenty of time, and proposed drifting leisurely mountainward, via the valley of San Jose, Pacheco Pass, and the plain of San Joaquin, and thence to Yosemite by any road that we chanced to find; enjoying the flowers and light, 'camping out' in our blankets wherever overtaken by night, and paying very little compliance to roads or times." He started the trip by taking a ferry to Oakland, and soon found nature in abundance.

Muir wrote: "We proceeded up the Santa Clara Valley to San Jose. It was the bloom-time of the year. The landscapes were fairly drenched with sunshine, all the air was quivering with the songs of the meadow-larks, and the hills were so covered with flowers that they seemed to be painted. Slow indeed was my progress through these glorious gardens, the first of the California flora I had seen."

Following John Muir's Footsteps

In the summer of 2005 Donna was backpacking the John Muir Trail (JMT) the 212-mile hiking route, named in Muir's honor, which travels along the crest of California's Sierra Nevada mountain range from Yosemite Valley to Mt. Whitney.

Donna was with a bunch of friends, Katy Sommer, David Worton, Tom Killion, and Jean Paul Cane, who are all veteran backpackers. They would hike and talk for hours, telling stories and making plans for future hikes. One day, just on the way out of Evolution Basin towards Muir Pass, talk turned to backpacking gear and food. Jean Paul said, "You know, John Muir would just grab a loaf of bread, put some tea in his pocket, throw a coat over his shoulder and walk to Yosemite…" It's the story we all have heard before. This time Donna heard something more in it, maybe it was a call from Muir in the wind whispering down the pass, and she said to everyone, "I want to do that. I'm going to step out my door and walk to Yosemite."

From the Back Cover

This book is really three books in one. It is a guidebook for a walking/cycling route across California that follows John Muir's footsteps from San Francisco to Yosemite via the Pacheco Pass. It is an adventure book, telling the story of Peter and Donna Thomas' 2006 ramble across California to discover that route. And finally it is a history book, presenting in its entirety and for the first time, the complete story of John Muir's first trip to Yosemite. That trip was taken in 1868, the year before Muir's "First Summer in the Sierra," and it has never been published before, existing in obscurity, in Muir's various writings, until it was reconstructed by Peter and Donna in preparation for their walk to Yosemite in his footsteps.

And So It Is   essays on the spiritual life
by Reverend James Fox

Happiness Is Thinking For One's Self
Happiness is a perfume you cannot pour on others without getting a few drops on yourself. Ralph Waldo Emerson

The observation one has of what is going on in the world is so depressing that people are asking; what has happened to the happiness in life? When one watches the evening news, and takes to heart what the talking head is saying, then one gets caught up in the doom and gloom that is the basis of a good news story.

One very seldom hears about the group that is helping the elders or the group that is raising funds to send a student in the community to a university for advanced studies that would create a person of high standards to represent the community. All of this seems to be part of the past and is no longer acted on by very many.

The lack of happiness has taken root and is growing in all areas of our society. The happiness one has in life starts within each being and is shared with others until there is a group who shares with each other and creates the happiness that fulfills the needs of everyone in the group.

The happiness one is looking for has to start within one's self while building your own little world around you with the happiness you desire. It seems like everyone expects the government to spread the happiness to all corners of the country, and when it doesn't happen the thought of failure by the government is what the talking heads of the news builds their stories on.

There isn't anyone in the world that can make one happy except one's self. The only person that can create happiness is the one who is searching for happiness. It all starts from the center of our being where the Creative Force of the Universe (God) dwells. Jesus referred to it as the Father within and said that it is the Father within that does the work for you in solving problems.

Since it is happiness most people are expecting, then it is

time they do the work on themselves to create the happiness they desire. The God of my understanding is always there ready to do whatever is asked of It in order to find the solution needed to solve whatever the problem may be.

Don't expect anything outside of yourself to create happiness in your life because nobody can create happiness for you. It is how you feel about yourself and your Creator and how you feel toward others that brings to you the love and happiness you desire.

Abraham Lincoln made a statement, "a person is as happy as they make up their minds to be." That is so true because it starts with the mindset one has as to what happiness is. The Local, State, or Federal Government cannot bring happiness into one's life if the person is not open to changing the things in their life to allow the Creative Force of the Universe (God) to create a happy life for them.

It is up to each person as to what to do to be happy because people are different in what makes them happy. The understanding of the spiritual energy dwelling within is the key to turning the lock that has been keeping all the good stuff locked out of one's life and it is up to the person as to when they want to turn the key.

The God of my understanding is there waiting to open the door when the key is turned and will pour the abundance of the Universe into one's life when they are open and willing to follow the direction of the God-Thoughts they get. Create your own world of happiness by recognizing the God that dwells within each being on this planet.

And So It Is.

A PARALLEL UNIVERSE TWO TALES OF PUBLIC FOLLY AND PERSONAL DEVASTATION
by Alex Landon & Elaine Halleck

Here is a unique bringing together of non-fiction (the lawyer's perspective) and fiction (the writer's view) on a topic of devastating concern to victims and the accused. Alex Landon (the lawyer) and Elaine Halleck (the writer) explore a particularly difficult topic; the effect of laws enacted in the aftermath of brutal child abductions and murders on those accused of lesser sexual crimes or those falsely accused, and the effect on society as a whole.

Introduction

In 2010, with the ink hardly dry on the first draft of this book, yet another clot of sexually motivated murders triggered a new aneurism in California's collective consciousness. The sorry and sordid killings of two teenagers, Chelsea King and Renee Dubois, evidenced uncanny similarities with the 2002 series of child abductions and killings that sparked the political mayhem that exiles people into the "parallel universe" detailed in these pages.

There was a striking similarity even in the seemingly minor matter of location: both Chelsea King and Danielle van Dam were killed in practically the same location in San Diego County near Poway. Other sociopolitical similarities seemed endless: the race—white—and photogenic qualities of the young victims; the eruption of public rage in the media; the active role taken by the victims' parents; the immediate appearance of proposed state laws named after the new victims; and the tired, toxic reactions of politicians such as County Supervisor Dianne Jacob, District Attorney Bonnie Dumanis, Governor Arnold Schwarzenegger and many others. Apparently these leaders had failed to learn a key lesson from earlier tragedies—that reacting to a crime with more repressive laws does not solve the problem—it actually makes it worse.

On the surface, the noxious political results of these two clusters of crimes in California—one cluster happening in 2002 and the other in 2010—seemed to spontaneously flow from their outrageous nature. However, at other times similar crimes occurring in faraway states had to be imported into California to be used as fodder for campaigns for more repressive laws. Such importation reveals how opportunistically tragic crimes are often used.

This happened midway between 2002 and 2010, in the 2006 push to pass "Jessica's law" as a voter initiative. Apparently, something in California's social and political mix seems to ensure that a horrible crime can always be found to promote the agenda of hateful or self-interested political forces who brew up destructive public policies. This apparent inexorability of "tsunami crimes" that devastate the sociopolitical landscape makes it seem as if the Summer of the Abducted White Girl is destined to be repeated again and again.

As that summer and its aftermath are detailed in this book, the reader will be taken on an unusual journey. Follow the fictionalized story of a man, his family and friends, and, in alternating chapters, look at the unfolding of dramatic social and political events that affected this individual and many others like him. In both trains of thought—particularly in the fictional story, but also in the political one—key details have been altered to make many of the people involved unrecognizable.

While Elaine Halleck's portion of the tale shows how policies of the criminal justice system might exile one person from any sustaining contact with his community and from any protection by civilizing principles that have evolved over the centuries, Alex Landon's non-fiction sections show how these policies have had severe effects on many other people and on the community at large. The ruinous expense of such policies is an important point in many of Landon's chapters.

It is not the authors' wish to discourage thoughtful readers with this sad story. Instead, we believe that it will inspire them to look beyond the headlines and see the lessons that must be learned from these tragedies. Once people gain a deeper understanding of the realities set forth in this book, we hope that they will seek out and support responsible solutions from leaders.

FROM ANCIENT ALIENS TO THE SHIFT:
THE GRAND UNIFIED THEORY
by Daniel D. Davis

Foreward (excerpts)

Let me start by saying unequivocally: I have never personally witnessed an Unidentified Flying Object (UFO). Despite that fact, however, several reasons motivated me to write this book. The principal cause is simply that the subject is so fascinating: While it may all come to nothing, merely more predictions that did not occur, the possibilities are truly astounding, and could signal a new age for humans. Another critical motivation is that I have yet to find any one source—book or film—that addresses the issue so succinctly and so comprehensively, that takes so many details into consideration, without being repetitive or appearing too hard to believe.

From a personal perspective, although I certainly never planned my life the way it has progressed, I am amazed at how many places I have visited or called home which figure prominently in accounts concerning UFOs. The first seven years of my life, for example, were spent in Santa Ana, California, where a significant, well-documented sighting of a flying saucer took place when I was one. My next home was in Ecuador, South America, which was once part of the Inca Empire, and there is a significant connection between extra-terrestrials and cultures in the area—particularly as regards their obsession with gold—while a certain cave in the southern part of the country is rumored to be a repository of alien knowledge. On our first furlough back to the States for summer vacation in 1974 we also visited Mexico, the same year in which there was a rash of UFO sightings in the country. One of the most memorable highlights of our visit was touring Teotihuacan, a site purportedly built with alien technology on a scale reflecting both our solar system and the alignment of particular stars.

. . .

Aspects of my own life and religious practices may also have a bearing on how the theories woven together in this book havedeveloped. For example, my involvement over the past year in sun gazing, where one harnesses the energy directly from the sun instead of eating so much food, led to a personal theory that I have not seen discussed in any of the works regarding extraterrestrials. Likewise, my family's traditional basis in Christianity has given me familiarity with the Bible that has been extremely useful in writing this book, although once out of my parent's home and not forced to go to church every Sunday and Wednesday, I realized that traditional religious explanations were not always the most logical. In the last year or two, in particular, I have seen mind-boggling displays of hypocrisy that have left me aghast at the claims made by some so-called religious people. Like a mathematical function, the more that someone quotes the Bible or loudly assert their beliefs, the more leery of such individuals I have grown to be.

Indeed, the evolution of my religious beliefs also predisposes me to consider the alternate views expressed in this book because my involvement in 'new thought' religions over the last few years also mirrors the potential spiritual progress of humanity. On a more global level, the actions taken by various countries over the last decade or so—especially ours—have left me dumbfounded. I believe the eighteenth-century British writer and politician, Soame Jenyns, said it best: "If Christian nations were nations of Christians, there would be no wars."

Likewise, due to what I have seen living around the world, and the extensive research I have done for various writing projects in the last few years, I have become keenly aware that our government does not always seem to have the best interests of all its citizens in mind. From the many founding fathers who owned slaves, to the documented lies used to start wars, to the meddling of corporations in politics, it is clear that our leaders have kept much from us throughout history. We will explore this topic as it relates specifically to the question of UFO sightings in great detail in chapter 3, because they certainly have reasons to keep the truth from us regarding alien visitations.

But, again: I have never personally seen a UFO. On the other hand, I know the earth is round even though I have never been in space to observe it personally, even though it looks flat from where I stand. So, while I hope that all the frightening possibilities will come to nothing—except, perhaps, a growth in human enlightenment and spirituality—as Louis Pasteur pointed out: "Chance favors the prepared mind."

A Citizen's Chronological History of World War II
Written daily from December 7, 1941 until August 14, 1945
by Shelton Kenneth Peterson

Foreward

The compilation of the historical record as it appears in the following pages was begun on December 7, 1941 and was finished three years, eight months, and seven days later on August 14, 1945.

As the bombs were falling on Pearl Harbor and as he (I) contemplated the dramatic impact of that "Day of Infamy" on the life of every human being, the author decided that it would be exceedingly interesting and perhaps valuable from an historical viewpoint, to record the course of the war as it unfolded chronologically in the life of one American citizen.

Accordingly, he (I) began compiling a daily record of the war as it was revealed through the mediums of newspapers, radio, and personal experiences; a daily record that was kept faithfully despite numerous obstacles ranging from eighty hours of grueling work each week during the early months of the war, to sickness and inertia. Many times the day's events were entered in the written record at two o'clock in the morning after a hectic day at the office or in bed when the "flu" laid him (me) low. Needless to say, the task seemed endless—the war would never be over—and then, as dramatically and suddenly as it began, came the atomic bomb and V-J Day.

As indicated in the opening article, the record contains many historical inaccuracies, but they are the inaccuracies that were part and parcel of the period involved. In other words, it is a picture of the war as it was currently presented to the people of the United States and as it was lived by one citizen of that nation. It is an historical record of a crucial period in the life of the Republic but it is not written in the dry, matter-of-fact manner of most histories. It is rather a living history, written in the present tense, in which you, as reader, can capture theatmosphere of the times. Through these pages you can re-live the war, day by day. In your mind you will hear once again the eerie wail of the air raid sirens and experience the helpless feeling of the blackout.

You will know the dreadful waiting and feel the desperate suspense over the outcome of crucial battles. You will realize more vividly than ever how fearful was our plight during those first one hundred days when the "gallopin' Jap" was rampaging over the vast reaches of the south seas. You will sense our will to conquer and glory in the courageous stand of our fighting men during those bleak days. You will glow with pride as you watch our power grow through the efforts of millions of patriotic Americans and will hang your head in shame and anger at the antics of the fearful who would hamstring the war effort.

Before you will pass a complete and unabridged panorama of the war, both on the home front and the battle front, a panorama that will lead you through all the valleys of despair and heartbreak that lay before this nation on that fateful December day in 1941. And when, at last, you live again through that tumultuous orgy of wild celebration that marked the end of the war, you will not only thank God that the ultimate victory was ours, but you will also be moved to offer a silent prayer that humanity may never again be called upon to suffer in so monstrous a manner.

Shelton Kenneth Peterson

December 7, 1941
San Francisco, California

Sunday, December 7, 1941: —WAR! WAR in the Pacific! Today, without warning, Japan struck at strategic American bases from the Philippines to Hawaii. News reports are confused, incoherent. Pearl Harbor attacked in great force. Wake Island captured. American transports sunk. Ships torpedoed only 700 miles at sea from San Francisco.

Thus, at 12:20 p.m. today, the news of the most treacherous attack in all American history broke the Sabbath quiet of the Nation. The complacent, strike-loving, peace seeking, yet unprepared American people were jolted with a sudden rush of anger to the realization that their hour had come. Now we shall see action! The President has called an emergency meeting of his cabinet and Congressional leaders; undoubtedly a declaration of war will follow in the morning. Censorship has been imposed. All military and naval leaves have been cancelled. Home guards are being mobilized. Civilians have been requested to enroll at their nearest fire department or police station. Mayor Rossi of San Francisco has issued a proclamation, declaring an emergency and demanding cessation of all strikes and disputes in order that a united front may face the uncertain future.

News bulletins flood in over the radio. Singapore is under attack. Thailand is invaded. Canada and the Dutch East Indies have declared war on Japan. Strangely enough Costa Rica has also jumped the gun with a declaration of war, evidently desiring to anticipate the United States' move. London seethes with excitement as the flame of WAR leaps with a great bound to encircle the earth. Washington boils with mounting anger and indignation at the treachery that brought the surprise attack while conversations for peace were still going on with Japan's special envoy, Kurusu. Hundreds are dying in Honolulu as orders are given throughout the Nation for production on a 24 hour basis. The San Francisco Bay region should be the seething, bustling center of this tragic Pacific war. Its great harbor, its important naval establishments, its mighty bridges, its aircraft factories, its industrial and financial nerve centers all combine to make it a first class objective for enemy attack, as well as a natural area of strategic importance. Already steps are being taken to put the entire district on a total war footing. Soldiers guard the bridges, FBI agents are rounding up the numerous Japanese aliens, and citizens are being mobilized.

From this vantage point, therefore, because the cause is so great, the outcome so uncertain, I shall attempt to make a chronological record of events as they come to me, an ordinary citizen, through the mediums of the radio, newspapers, and personal experiences. For this reason the record will reflect all the propaganda, rumors, and inaccuracies which abound in those mediums. But it will show the picture as it is lived day by day in the midst of a terrible and fascinating moment in history. Thus it may prove interesting and of some historical value. So, until tomorrow, may God be with our beloved Country.

August 14, 1945

Tuesday, August 14, 1945:—IT'S HERE! THE UNBELIEVABLE, UNFORGETTABLE, GREATEST DAY IN HISTORY! WORLD WAR II IS OVER! THE GRAVEST CALAMITY EVER TO BEFALL MANKIND HAS COME TO AN END AT LONG LAST. THE CAUSE OF FREE MEN HAS AGAIN TRIUMPHED. GOD BLESS AMERICA! GOD BLESS THE UNITED NATIONS!

I can hardly write this record. It is now 11:30 p.m. and crowded events of this hectic day are racing through my mind so that words are hard to hog-tie and throw on to paper. You would have to live through it to even imagine it. You would have to elbow your way as I have through the indescribable, milling throng on Market Street in downtown San Francisco, join with the shouting, cheering, back-slapping, delirious sailors who jam packed the sidewalks and spilled over into the middle of the street from the famous old Ferry Building on up as far as the eye could reach. It was a scene of utter abandon, of swirling confetti and ticker tape, of wild eyed soldiers, sailors, and marines hilariously mobbing any girl who dared to brave the gauntlet and smothering her with kisses, their lips ruby red from previous conquests. Civilians and servicemen alike gave way completely before the wave of pent up emotions that tore down the barriers of restraint built up over almost four long years of war. Wearing apparel was exchanged. Soldiers were wearing women's hats and civilian's ties. One Lieutenant was togged out in a civilian's hat, a woman's scarf, and high heel shoes. Even I lost my Stetson and tie and ended up by wearing a sailor's little white hat and black tie. In short, it was a superlative demonstration of insane joy—and relief. And yet, with it all, there was an undertone—or overtone if you will—of sadness—sadness for the boys who will not come home—sadness for those families that will forever bear a bitter scar reminding them of the terrible conflict just ended. The peal of sacred bells and the quiet, open doors of churches, through which filed a more somber group, told of the other side to this great celebration.

The day began quietly enough, despite the air of tense expectancy that everyone has been wearing the last two days. It was not until shortly after 4 p.m. that the official news broke. Before pandemonium was unleashed, we were able to find out that President Truman had called the newsmen into his office at 4 p.m. and formally announced the receipt of Japan's acceptance of unconditional surrender. General Douglas MacArthur was named Supreme Allied Commander to receive the Japanese surrender and all Allied armed forces were ordered to suspend offensive action. Thus it ended, just three years, eight months, and seven days after the "day that will live in infamy," December 7, 1941. And with this day we come to the end of this record. What happens from tomorrow on is another story, a story of great importance no doubt, but a story of peace. This record has been a story of war. Through its pages we have lived the greatest conflict in the bloody history of mankind. Little did we know that terrible eon ago when we began this daily record where it would lead us, through what valleys of despair, what rivers of "blood, toil, sweat, and tears" before this great day would come. As we look back over that tortuous pathway, bitter though it was, we silently offer a prayer. God was guiding us. Our land, through His grace, was spared the rain of death and destruction visited upon less fortunate lands. Through His grace, and the sturdy backs and courageous hearts of America's sons and daughters we have won "the inevitable triumph" and redeemed the pledge so solemnly made by President Roosevelt that tragic day so long ago. Let us pray to God in this triumphant hour that He may continue to guide this land and this people in the days to come so that we may lead the world to that glorious goal for which mankind has sacrificed so much— a lasting peace, with prosperity and happiness for all.

The End

ON FREEDOM: ORGANIZATIONAL SCIENCE EXAMINED PHILOSOPHICALLY
By Peter Gibson Friesen

from the Preface

There is something pleasant in the realization that upon the completion of writing an abstract and contemplative treatise I am tasked to write a "preface" so that others might track with the development of its argument. It thus extends as a gesture of good will from a perspective which was once reflective and insular, now changed by the prospect that others could trouble themselves to understand what these five essays on freedom mean.

Not that they necessarily "mean" anything, or that I might change what they are through insertion. It might help, nonetheless, for me to share what motivated the devotion of many years of labor to this task.

This work did not start as a treatise on freedom, but rather, as a fascination with discoveries of "fact" about human institutions. These discoveries occurred within a movement of research occurring over the latter half of the twentieth century. It was once called "stratified systems theory" by its progenitor Elliott Jaques (deceased 2003), because of its focus on "hierarchy" in management structures. It later became "requisite organization" as the research matured into a systematic comment on the "health" of bureaucratic structures. The name "requisite" signified a move from organization as something imposed on human nature to something that agrees with it.

The "facts" unearthed within this movement were remarkable, revealing consistancy in the way human collaborative endeavors organize hierarchically—across all contexts of law, economic production, institutional output and culture. These facts spawned a generation of theory, not just about what human organization is, but about what human beings are. We are, it seems, engaged in stages of growth, and we experience fairly predictable changes in the way we solve problems. These changes represent progressive improvement of control over one's work environment, and thus do much to account for the development of hierarchy in human institutions. I have given some thought to the explanation of how and why this happens, and have written it down.

On Freedom: Organizational Science Examined Philosophically

Contents

Preface

1. Scientific Freedom

2. Intellectual Freedom

3. Moral Freedom

4. Political Freedom

5. Spiritual Freedom

Postscript

Appendix: The system of notation that marks the contours of a Logic of Maturation

LISTING OF ALL POETIC MATRIX PRESS TITLES
AND IMPRINTS (PM BOOKS, PM LIBRARY, KVASIR BOOKS)
BY PUBLISHING DATE; WITH AUTHOR BIOGRAPHY

POETIC MATRIX PRESS

2017
SPOKES OF DREAM OR BIRD, BY PATRICIA NELSON, *(POETRY)*

Patricia Nelson is a semi-retired attorney and environmentalist. She has worked with the "Activist" group of poets in California for many years. The group rose to brief prominence in the 1940s and 50s and is now undergoing a resurgence of publication by a different generation of poets. The Activist credo is that every word in a poem should be poetically "active," employing some kind of focused poetic technique—a principle not as self-evident as it might sound. The group often works with metaphoric imagery.

RIVER LIGHT, BY CHRIS OLANDER *(POETRY)*

Chris Olander has worked as a landscaper, laborer, floral farmer and designer, Poet/Teacher. Chris has been writing poetry since 1984, "Articulating artistic words through music, spoken word and gestures: poetry experiences of energized body language." Olander's poetry arises from land-based ethics rooted in science, observation and reflection. "I explore human horrors and beautiful auras of mystical revelations and all that is possible in being here now. What we make of life is what we get. I create an action art poetry: musical image phrasing to dramatize relative experiences—a poetry from oral and bard traditions, a sound poet exploring meanings, ideas and emotions in rhythm patterns."

Olander has worked as a Poet/Teacher with California Poets in Schools (CPITS) since 1984. He teaches and reads his work throughout California and in Oregon, Washington and Hawaii. He has been published in many anthologies, magazines and specialty publications. Olander was a founding director of Poet's Playhouse in Nevada City, 1988-99; Nevada County Poetry Series of Grass Valley, 2000-12; an organizer and featured reader for the Berkeley Watershed Environmental Poetry Festival since 2001.

THE NATURE OF MOUNTAINS, BY JOHN (PETERSON), KVASIR BOOKS *(POETRY)*

John (Peterson) is the author of five previous books of poetry including chapbooks This Warrior is always at Peace and Uzumite;full volumes News of the Day, dark hills and wild mountains and Two Races One Face Two Faces One Race with Tomás Gayton. John is the publisher and editor of Poetic Matrix Press and Poetic Matrix Press' online Forever Journal and Poets Comment into the World blogs. As the publisher of Poetic Matrix Press, a literary small press, he has published 60 books of poetry and prose from writers across the country and around the world. He has read from his poetry, lectured and taught at: the University of California San Diego; California State University San Diego; California State University Fresno; University for Humanistic Studies, Del Mar, CA; The Writing Center in San Diego; Palomar College San Marcos; Merced High School; Yosemite National Park including the Yosemite Centennial Celebration at the Ahwahnee Hotel in 1990. Information on Poetic Matrix Press can be found at www.poeticmatrix.com.

The Benign Tree, by Richard Kovac, Kvasir Books *(Poetry)*

Richard Kovac was born in 1944 in Newark, New Jersey into a working class immigrant family and raised by the Italian side of it after the death of his father in 1946. He attended Fairleigh Dickinson University at the Rutherford campus, graduating in 1965, and attended graduate school at the nearby Montclair State College. He has been a civil servant in four states (at different times on the municipal, county, state, and federal levels), a teacher, and an import cost clerk. He is married (1979) to Elizabeth and they have a daughter named Pax, which means 'peace' in Latin, but is pronounced to rhyme with 'ax.'

Richard has been a member of the peace movement since 1965, in particular the War Resisters League and the Catholic Worker Movement founded by Peter Maurin and Dorothy Day. He published a chapbook based on his experience called, *Down and Out in Waukegan and Wisconsin*. His full length books, *Untitled* and *Wheels within Wheels*, were published by PM Books an imprint of Poetic Matrix Press in 2008 and 2011. The author and his family live in Stevens Point, Wisconsin.

Spiraling Forward: A Dance Through the Cycles of Life, by Ashley Gene Pinkerton *(Poetry)*

Ashley Gene Pinkerton is a writer, poet and practitioner who specializes in Reiki and Shamanic Energy Medicine. She has studied the indigenous wisdom traditions of South America through The Four Winds Society, Institute of Energy Medicine and is a Reiki Master/Teacher of the Usui System of Natural Healing. As a facilitator, she assists her clients and students in finding a greater depth of alignment with their own personal power and innate ability to heal.

Ashley's own spiritual awakening in 2012 was the catalyst which allowed her to transform her life, giving her a deeper understanding of herself and her interconnectedness to all things of creation. She finds great strength and inspiration in her connection to Mother Earth and Spirit, and all that she writes about is brought forth from this connection and from the higher perspective she views life from.

The Forgotten Shore, by J. P. Linstroth *(Poetry)*

J. P. Linstroth is an Adjunct Professor at Barry University. He is the author of the book: Marching Against Gender Practice: Political Imaginings in the Basqueland (2015, Lexington Books). He obtained a D.Phil. (PhD) in Social and Cultural Anthropology from the University of Oxford with several awards for his research concentrating on the Spanish-Basques. Linstroth was a recipient of two travel grants from the Basque regional government to speak on issues of peace and conflict resolution in the Basque Country (2005 & 2006) and a signatory of the Brussels Declaration for Peace to end ETA violence (2010). He was a co-recipient of an Alexander von Humboldt Foundation Grant (2005-2007) to study immigrant populations in South Florida, Cubans, Haitians, with particular emphasis on Guatemalan-Mayan immigrants. Furthermore, he was awarded a J. William Fulbright Foreign Scholar Grant (2008-2009) to study urban Amerindians in Manaus, Brazil and to be a Visiting Professor with the Department of Anthropology at the Universidade Federal do Amazonas (UFAM). His main academic research interests are: cognition, ethnonationalism, gender, genocide, history, immigrant advocacy, indigeneity, indigenous politics, indigenous rights, memory, peace, peacebuilding, racism, and trauma. Linstroth is also an artist. His paintings have been shown at various venues in Palm Beach and Martin Counties, Florida. The Forgotten Shore (2017, Poetic Matrix Press) is Linstroth's first book of poetry.

2016

On Freedom: Organizational Science Examined Philosophically, by Peter Gibson Friesen, PM Library *(Non-Fiction)*

Peter Friesen received his Bachelor of Arts from Williams College in 1978, majoring in Philosophy. He continued to pursue his philosophical interests in Public Administration at the University of Southern California, and a Juris Doctorate at the University of California, Hastings, awarded in 1982. While a student at the University of Southern California he studied with Elliot Jaques and played a major role in the development of the first logical descriptors for cognitive development utilizing an information processing model.

STRINGS OF SHINING SILENCE EARTH-LOVE POEMS, BY RAPHAEL BLOCK *(POETRY)*

Raphael Block was born on a kibbutz in Israel to pioneering parents and spent his boyhood playing on the hills of Haifa.

Just before turning nine, his family returned to London. Learning English shaped his ear for sounds, and the British climate and temperament fashioned his life over the next 25 years, until he met and married an American living in London.

In 1993 they moved to Northern California with their daughter. His partner died from cancer in 2002, and for the following years he feels it was his privilege to raise their child.

Raphael has worked with children of all ages for almost 30 years. A long time meditator, he breathes in wonder at the earth's and our own rhythmic ebb and flow. He dwells in an old apple orchard outside of Sebastopol, and is often accompanied by musicians when performing.

COMPOSING TEMPLE SUNRISE: OVERCOMING WRITER'S BLOCK AT BURNING MAN, BY HASSAN EL-TAYYAB *(MEMOIR)*

Hassan El-Tayyab is an award-winning singer/songwriter, author, teacher, and political organizer. His critically-acclaimed Americana act *American Nomad* performs regularly at festivals and venues up and down the West Coast and beyond. In addition to performing Hassan is also a music educator, having taught songwriting and guitar classes for the *Freight and Salvage* and *The East Bay Center for the Performing Arts*. Hassan has also been a guest lecturer on songwriting at the University of California, Berkeley. You can follow Hassan and his music at www.americannomadmusic.com.

2015

BLACK KRIPPLE DELIVERS POETRY & LYRICS, BY LEROY FRANKLIN MOORE, JR. *(POETRY & LYRICS)*

Leroy F. Moore, Jr. is a Black writer, poet, hip-hop\music lover, community activist and feminist with a physical disability. Leroy formed one of the first organizations for people of color with disabilities in the San Francisco Bay Area that lasted five years in the late 90s. He is one of the founding members of the National Black Disability Coalition. Leroy was co-host of a radio show in San Francisco at KPOO 89.5 FM, and Berkeley at KPFA 94.1 FM. He has studied, worked and lectured in the field of race and disability concerning blues, hip-hop, and social justice issues in the United States, United Kingdom, Canada and South Africa. Leroy is currently writing a Krip-Hop book, about Hip-Hop artists with disabilities from around the world. Leroy has won many awards for his advocacy from the San Francisco Mayor's Disability Council under Willie L. Brown to the Local Hero Award in 2002 from Public Television Station, KQED in San Francisco.

Leroy has interviewed hip-hop\soul\blues\jazz artists with disabilities: the Blind Boys of Alabama, Jazz elder Jimmy Scott, Hip-Hop star Wonder Mike of the Sugar Hill Gang, DJ Quad of LA, Paraplegic MC of Chicago, Rob DA Noize Temple of New York; Hip-Hop journalists like Greg Tate, Billy Jam and Harry Allen to name a few. Leroy is a longtime columnist with one of the first columns on race & disability started in the early 90's at Poor Magazine in San Francisco.

THE ART OF HEALING, BY GAIL AND CHARLES ENTREKIN
(POETRY)

Gail Rudd Entrekin is Poetry Editor of Hip Pocket Press and Editor of the online environmental literary magazine, *Canary* (www.canarylitmag.org). She is Editor of the poetry anthology *Yuba Flows (2007) and* the poetry & short fiction anthology *Sierra Songs & Descants: Poetry & Prose of the Sierra (2002).*

Her poems have been widely published in anthologies and literary magazines, including Cimarron Review, Nimrod, New Ohio Review, and Southern Poetry Review, were finalists for the Pablo Neruda Prize in Poetry from Nimrod International Journal in 2011, and won the Women's National Book Association Award in 2016.

Gail taught poetry and English literature at California colleges for 25 years. Her books of poetry include *The Art of Healing* with Charles Entrekin, Poetic Matrix Press, 2016; *Rearrangement of the Invisible*, Poetic Matrix Press, 2012; *Change (will do you good)*, Poetic Matrix Press, 2005, which was nominated for a Northern California Book Award; *You Notice the Body*, Hip Pocket Press, 1998; and *John Danced*, Berkeley Poets

Workshop & Press, 1983. She and her husband, poet and novelist Charles Entrekin, live in the hills of San Francisco's East Bay.

Charles Entrekin's most recent works include *The Art of Healing, a transformative poetic journey*, Poetic Matrix Press, 2016; *Portrait of a Romance*, a love story in verse, Hip Pocket Press, 2014. Charles was a founder and managing editor of The Berkeley Poets Cooperative and The Berkeley Poets Workshop & Press, and was a co-founder/advisory board member of Literature Alive!, a non-profit organization in Nevada County, California. He is co-editor of the e-zine Sisyphus, a magazine of literature, philosophy, and culture; and managing editor of Hip Pocket Press. Charles is the father of five children and lives in the San Francisco Bay Area with his wife, poet Gail Rudd Entrekin.

Borderless Butterflies: Earth Haikus and Other Poems / Mariposas sin fronteras: Haikus terrenales y otros poemas, BY FRANCISCO ALARCÓN *(POETRY)*

Francisco X. Alarcón, award-winning poet and educator, was born in Los Angeles, grew up in Guadalajara, Mexico, and lived in Davis, where he taught at the University of California. He is the author of twelve volumes of poetry, including *Canto hondo / Deep Song*, University of Arizona Press, 2015; *Ce • Uno • One: Poems for the New Sun*, Swan Scythe Press, 2010.

Francisco is the author of four acclaimed books of bilingual poems for children on the seasons of the year originally published by Children's Book Press, now an imprint of Lee & Low Books: *Laughing Tomatoes and Other Spring Poems* (1997), *From the Bellybutton of the Moon and Other Summer Poems* (1998), *Angels Ride Bikes and Other Fall Poems* (1999), and *Iguanas in the Snow and Other Winter Poems* (2001). He published two other bilingual books for children with Lee & Low Books: *Poems to Dream Together* (2005) and *Animal Poems of the Iguazú* (2008). He received numerous literary awards and prizes for his works, including the American Book Award, the Pen Oakland Josephine Miles Award, the Chicano Literary Prize, the Fred Cody Lifetime Achievement Award, the Jane Adams Honor Book Award, and several Pura Belpré Honor Book Awards by the American Library Association. In 1993, he co-founded *Los Escritores del Nuevo Sol* / Writers of the New Sun, a collective of writers based in Sacramento, California. He was the creator of the Facebook page "Poets Responding to SB 1070." Francisco passed on 15 January 2016 at age 61, he is missed by many.

Spangling Darkness, by Raphael Block *(Poetry)*
for bio see *Strings of Shining Silence Earth-Love Poems*

Malala, by Lyn Lifshin *(Poetry)*
Lyn Lifshin has written more than 125 books and edited 4 anthologies of women writers. Her poems have appeared in most poetry and literary magazines in the U.S.A, and her work has been included in virtually every major anthology of recent writing by women. She has given more than 700 readings across the U.S.A. and has appeared at Dartmouth and Skidmore colleges, Cornell University, the Shakespeare Library, Whitney Museum, and Huntington Library. Lyn Lifshin has also taught poetry and prose writing for many years at universities, colleges and high schools, and has been Poet in Residence at the University of Rochester, Antioch, and Colorado Mountain College. Winner of numerous awards including the Jack Kerouac Award for her book *Kiss The Skin Off*, Lyn is the subject of the documentary film *Lyn Lifshin: Not Made of Glass*. For her absolute dedication to the small presses which first published her, and for managing to survive on her own apart from any major publishing house or academic institution, Lifshin has earned the distinction "Queen of the Small Presses." She has been praised by Robert Frost, Ken Kesey and Richard Eberhart, and Ed Sanders has seen her as "a modern Emily Dickinson."

Landscape of a Woman and a Hummingbird, by Joseph Milosch *(Poetry)*
Joseph Milosch graduated in 1995 with his MFA from San Diego State University. He has published poetry and essays in various magazines, and has had multiple nominations for the Pushcart Award. His first book *The Lost Pilgrimage Poems* was published by Poetic Matrix Press.

He has published in many journals over the years. He received an Excellence in Literature award from Mira Costa College.

His first chapbook, *On the Wing*, was published by Barnes and Noble as a regional publication, and his second chapbook, *Father of Boards and Woodwinds*, was published by the Inevitable Press for the Laguna Poets Series. He was a finalist in the Tennessee Middle State Chapbook contest in 1996 for his chapbook, *If I Could Imagine*. He won the 1997 Tennessee Middle State Chapbook contest with his chapbook *Among Men*. In 1999 The Laguna Poets Series published his fourth chapbook *Now She Bends Away* with Inevitable Press.

2014
I AM HOMELAND - TWELVE KOREAN-AMERICAN POETS, EDITED BY YEARN HONG CHOI *(POETRY)*
for bio see *Song of Myself: A Korean-American Life*

A CITIZEN'S CHRONOLOGICAL HISTORY OF WORLD WAR II, BY SHELTON KENNETH PETERSON, PM LIBRARY *(NON-FICTION)*
Shelton Kenneth Peterson was born on 1 February 1911 to Minnie Lee Harkin and Charles Mauritz Peterson in Salt Lake City Utah. In (high school) ROTC he became a captain and received a medal for marksmanship. He graduated from high school at 17 years old and took a job with the Federal Reserve Bank in Salt Lake City. He began as a messenger boy and when he passed away in 1970 was a Department Head of Bonds and Redemption. He worked for them for 42 years. Early in 1941 he received a promotion at the bank and they moved to San Francisco, California. On December 7, 1941 the Japanese attacked Pearl Harbor in Hawaii and that is when he decided to chronicle the war. This volume was published postumously.

2013
KOHL & CHALK, BY SHADAB ZEEST HASHMI *(POETRY)*
Shadab Zeest Hashmi, author of *Kohl and Chalk* and *Baker of Tarifa*, is the recipient of the San Diego Book Award, the Nazim Hikmet Prize, and multiple Pushcart nominations. Her work has been translated into Spanish and Urdu, and has appeared in *Prairie Schooner, Mudlark, The Cortland Review, Poetry International, Vallum, POEM, The Adirondack Review, Spillway, Atlanta Review, Journal of PostcolonialWritings,Wasafiri, Rhino, Nimrod, Drunken Boat, Asymptote* and other journals worldwide. She has taught in the MFA program at San Diego State University as a writer-in-residence and has presented in Turkey, Spain, Pakistan, Mexico, the UK and the U.S.

SOJOURN ON THE BOHEMIAN HIGHWAY, BY TOMÁS GAYTON *(POETRY / MEMOIR)*
Tomás Gayton was born and raised in Seattle, Washington, the grandson of African American pioneers. He began writing verse soon after graduating with a Juris Doctor from the University of Washington. Tomás

is a retired Civil Rights attorney/activist, teacher and world traveler who lives in San Diego. His poetry is his life in verse.

Tomás' words have appeared in PoetsWest, The Seattle Review, Vision Magazine, The San Diego Reader, City Works, African American Review and other literary publications. His most recent volume of poetry and prose is *Sojourn on the Bohemian Highway*, published by Poetic Matrix Press. His memoir, Long Journey Home, is available through the Amazon Kindle Store. Other works include: *Vientos de Cambio / Winds of Change*, *Yazoo City Blues*, *Time of the Poet*, *Dark Symphony in Duet* with the late Sarah Fabio, and *Two Races, One Face,* with John Peterson. Tomás' work is also featured on his website (www.sambajia.com).

Rabbit Stories, by Kim Shuck *(poetic fiction)*

Kim Shuck is a poet, weaver, educator, doer of piles of laundry, planter of seeds, traveler and child wrangler. She was born in her mother's hometown of San Francisco, one hill away from where she now lives. Her ancestors were and are Tsalagi, Sauk and Fox and Polish, for the most part. She earned a Master of Fine Arts degree in weaving in 1998 from San Francisco State University.

As a poet Kim has read her work around the US and elsewhere. In late 2005 she toured through Jordan with a group of poets from all over the globe in the interest of peace and communication. Shuck reads her work on local radio frequently.

Kim's visual art has been included in shows both locally and abroad such as a textile show at the National Museum of Taiwan in Taipei and Art, Women, California at the San Jose Art Museum. She consults with museums and galleries around California on the subjects of Native artwork and community inclusion.

Kim continues working in schools and has taught at all levels: at San Francisco State University as well as many elementary schools. Her work with the Exploratorium, a hands on museum in San Francisco, is included in that museum's "Across Cultures" series. She's been teaching since 3rd grade when she organized and taught a class on crochet. Her work generally touches on poetry, art, math, storytelling, humor, and whatever else seems useful at the time.

Kim was named the 2017 San Francisco Poet Laureate. She resides in the extraordinary company that came before.

2012
Rearrangement of the Invisible, by Gail Rudd Entrekin *(poetry)*
for bio see *The Art of Healing*

Light in All Directions, poems by Brandon Cesmat *(poetry)*
Brandon Cesmat teaches literature & writing at several colleges in Southern California. His first book, *Driven into the Shade,* received a San Diego Book Award. His short story collection *When Pigs Fall in Love & Other Stories* is from Caernarvon Press. He is an active teaching artist in California Poets in the Schools (CPITS) and an active member in Teaching Artists Organize (TAO).

Whimsy, Reticence & Laud: Unruly Sonnets, by Grace Marie Grafton *(poetry)*
Grace Marie Grafton is the author of four previous collections of poetry. *Zero* won the 2000 Poetic Matrix Chapbook Contest. *Visiting Sisters* is a collection inspired by the artwork of contemporary women. *Other Clues* consists of experimental prose poems. Her recent chapbook, *Chrysanthemum Oratorio,* plays with concept and language.

Ms. Grafton has taught for many years in the California Poets In The Schools program, for which she was awarded twelve California Arts Council grants. She was named Teacher of the Year by the River Of Words annual student poetry contest co-sponsored by Robert Hass, United States Poet Laureate.

Born and raised in California's central valley, she lives in Oakland with her husband, Michael, and their extended family.

Trial and Error: The Education of a Freedom Lawyer—Volume Three: Return to the Defense, by Law Professor Arthur W. Campbell *(poetic prose)*
Art Campbell was born in Brooklyn, raised in Appalachia, and scholarshipped to Harvard and Georgetown Universities. Prior to earning his second law degree he was a road-maintenance worker, janitor, boxer, rugby player, and professional musician. He became a trial lawyer for and against the government in Washington, D.C., where he also supervised students in the D.C. Law Students In Court program.

Campbell later moved to San Diego, became a tenured professor at California Western School of Law, and authored the country's definitive treatise on criminal sentencing. Married to the best-selling novelist Drusilla Campbell, they raised two sons and have enjoyed training large dogs and horses.

From Ancient Aliens to the Shift: The Grand Unified Theory, by Daniel D. Davis, PM Library (NON-FICTION)

Daniel D. Davis is trained in mathematics and brings his skills as a researcher to his writing. Growing up in Ecuador he has lived on five continents, been to 36 countries, and lived and taught in the Congo, Romania, and Pakistan. His life as an adventurer found him B.A.S.E. jumping, skydiving, paragliding, hang gliding, scuba diving, rappelling, bungee-jumping, snowboarding, and skateboarding. With training in martial arts, he is also an accomplished guitarist and singer. His fascination with the world and the peoples and cultures he has known also informs his current work.

Triumph At Last: A Korean-American Life, by Steven Soo Hyun Kim, PM Library (MEMOIR, WITH PHOTOS)

Steven Soo Hyun Kim's memoir relates growing up in poverty-stricken Korea in the 40s and 50s, and his life during Korea's drive toward modernization, and then during the Vietnam War in the 1960s, and finally to his life in the United States of America as a civil engineer. He contributed to the city of Atlanta as a civil engineer. His projects included drafting and constructing Atlanta's waste water plant; constructing the 70-story Peachtree Plaza Hotel; and Georgia Tech's Urban Life Center and gym. He Lives in Marietta, Georgia

2011
Realization Point, by Chris Hoffman (POETRY)

Chris Hoffman is a poet and ecopsychologist with a background in organization development (applied group psychology) and counseling. In addition to *Realization Point* with Poetic Matrix Press, Chris is the author of two other volumes of poetry, *Cairns* and *On the Way*, and a nonfiction work on ecopsychology and spirituality: *The Hoop and the Tree: A Compass for Finding a Deeper Relationship with All Life*. His poetry has appeared in national journals including *Appalachia, The Christian Science Monitor, The Climbing Art, Sea Kayaker, Spiritus, Sufi Journal,* and *The Chrysalis Reader,* and also in the anthologies *The Soul Unearthed* and *EarthLight: Spiritual Wisdom for an Ecological Age.*

As a consultant and counselor Chris has facilitated human and organization development in a variety of business, educational, and therapeutic settings, recently specializing in organizations working for a sustainable future. He now devotes most of his time to poetry and to volunteer work related to keeping a livable climate.

Chris is a long-time student of Zen and T'ai Chi and is interested in traditional healing practices and sacred dance. His wilderness experience includes backpacking, mountaineering, and river running. He lives with his wife in Boulder, Colorado. They have one son. (More information at www.hoopandtree.org.)

TOWARD THE HELIOPAUSE, BY JOAN MICHELSON *(POETRY)*

Joan Michelson won first prize in the Bristol Poetry Competition, UK, 2015, first prize in the Torriano Competition, UK, 2014, and she received the Hamish Canham prize from the Poetry Society of England, 2012 and her poem 'Self-Portrait with Secret' was a Poetry Society newsletter selection Dec 2016. Her writing has been selected for several British Council and Arts Council anthologies of New Writing. Her first collection, Toward the Heliopause was published by Poetic Matrix Press, CA, USA, 2011. Her chapbook, Bloomvale Home, portraits of residents in a care home, by Original Plus Books, UK, 2016. Forthcoming, 2017, from Sentinel Books, UK, a new collection, Landing Stage. Forthcoming 2018, from The Finishing Line Press, KY, chapbook, 'The Family Kitchen'. Originally from New England, USA, Joan lives in London, England.

LISTENING: NEW & SELECTED WORK, BY CHARLES ENTREKIN *(POETRY)*

for bio see Art of Healing

WHEELS WITHIN WHEELS BY RICHARD KOVAC, PM BOOKS *(POETRY)*

for bio see *The Benign Tree*

A Parallel Universe: Two Tales of Public Folly and Personal Devastation, by Alex Landon and Elaine Halleck PM Library *(non-fiction/fiction)*
Alex Landon is an attorney specializing in criminal law. He is an adjunct professor at the University of San Diego School of Law, teaching Corrections and Sentencing for 26 years; past president of California Attorneys for Criminal Justice and the San Diego Criminal Defense Bar Association; and former Executive Director of the Defenders Program of San Diego, Inc. He is a frequent speaker at seminars and public programs.
Elaine Halleck is a journalist, graphic designer and linguist. She has contributed to publications including the (Detroit) Metro Times, the Tokyo Journal, the Sacramento News and Review and the Guadalajara Reporter.

2010
Baker of Tarifa, by Shadab Zeest Hashmi *(poetry)*
Winner of the 2011 San Diego Book Award for poetry, and nominated for a Pushcart Prize.
for bio see *Kohl & Chalk*

The Postman, by Korean poet Mun Dok-su
(poetry with three commentaries)
Mun Dok-su, famed poet, scholar, former president of the Korea PEN, and a member of the Korean Academy of Arts, was born in Haman, South Kyungsang Province, graduated from Hongik University (B.A.), and Korea University (M.A. and Ph.D.). He taught at Hongik University from 1961 until his retirement. His major field was Korean Literature. He also taught at Seoul National University, Korea University and Yonsei University.

Since 1955, the year he began to write poems, Mun has published 19 books of poems, 10 books of critical essays, 3 books of miscellaneous essays. *Study of Korean Modernistic Poetry* ('81), *Theory of Poetry* ('93) are his major books of criticism. *Ecstasy* ('56) is his first book of poems, and *Line/Space* ('66), the second book of poems, together with his thesis "Aesthetics of the Inner World" (Mar. 1966, *Sasanggye*), is regarded as a pioneering achievement of Korean modernism, which claims poetic liberty and the principle of free construction of imagery in the conscious

POETIC MATRIX PRESS

TRIAL AND ERROR: THE EDUCATION OF A FREEDOM LAWYER—VOLUME TWO: FOR THE PROSECUTION, BY LAW PROFESSOR ARTHUR W. CAMPBELL *(POETIC PROSE)*
for bio see *TRIAL and ERROR Volume III*

SONG OF MYSELF: A KOREAN-AMERICAN LIFE, BY YEARN HONG CHOI *(MEMOIR WITH PHOTOS)*
Yearn Hong Choi received his undergraduate degree in public administration from Yonsei University and his master's and doctorate degree in political science (public administration) from Indiana University. He taught at the University of Wisconsin and Old Dominion University, and worked in the Office of the Secretary of Defense (1981-1983) as an assistant for environmental quality (NASPAA Fellow) before returning to Korea. He is a retired professor and chairman of the environmental policy program at the University of Seoul Graduate School of Urban Sciences, and a member of the Presidential Commission on Sustainable Development. His name is listed in *World Who Is Who and Does What in Environment and Conservation* (Geneva, Switzerland). He contributed to *Encyclopedia of Modern Asia* (USA) in the Korean environmental affairs.

TIMEWINDS, BY LEE UNDERWOOD, PM BOOKS *(POETRY)*
Lee Underwood As a lead guitarist living in L.A. during the Sixties and early Seventies, Lee Underwood toured and recorded with singer and songwriter Tim Buckley for seven years. In 2004, he published *Blue Melody: Tim Buckley Remembered* (Backbeat, San Francisco), honored by Britain's *Uncut* music magazine as one of the ten best music books of the year. In 1990, Underwood co-authored flutist Paul Horn's autobiography, *Inside Paul Horn* (HarperCollins), and received the Crystal Award for Music Journalism. He completed his lengthy novel, *Diamondfire: The Journey*, in 2005, and continues to write essays, poetry, and short stories while living with his wife in a modern cabin near Yosemite National Park, California.

MINDSCAPE UNLOCKED? BY ADAM FUNK, PM BOOKS *(POETRY)*
Adam Funk received a Bachelor's Degree in 2008 from the University of Nevada, Las Vegas. He is an advocate for the handicapped. His cerebral palsy has made him more aware of the vast changes that need to be

made in public places – like schools. His interests include reading, writing, watching movies, and playing video games.

A Rose in the Briar Patch, by Dan Tharp, PM Books
(POETRY)

Dan Tharp - This is Dan's fourth publication. "Side by Side," "Yielding Desire to Fate," and "A Season Made for Wandering" were published in chapbook form, through Shadowpoetry.com. Dan was born and raised in Western Oklahoma. He now resides in North San Diego County.

Muir Ramble Route: A Guide for Hiking from San Francisco to Yosemite, by Peter & Donna Thomas
(TRAVEL NON-FICTION - HIKING GUIDE WITH INTERIOR PHOTOS, DRAWINGS, & MAPS)

Peter & Donna Thomas grew up next to open spaces. "We spent much of our early childhoods outdoors, hiking, exploring, wading in creeks, climbing in trees and over rocks. Donna's parents were Scout leaders and she grew up backpacking, my parents took me surfing. To be really honest, as a kid I watched my share of TV. We are both just regular folks. Throughout our lives we have continued to backpack, camp and be in love with the outdoors, in fact Donna has hiked the John Muir Trail twice, but we did not grow up to be professional adventurers, biologists or naturalists.

"We ended up as book artists. I make paper and have an old letterpress with lots of metal type. Donna uses pen and watercolors to paint words and images. Together we create one-of-a-kind and limited edition books. We know how to make artist's books, but found writing this guidebook a challenge and have many people to thank.

Like Fallen Snow: Memoir with Poetry, by Ruth Rosenthal (PM Books) *(POETRY/MEMOIR)*

Ruth Rosenthal put aside a scholarship to Newark State College, in New Jersey, before making California her home. Twenty years later, after taking all the available non-credited writing classes she could find, Ruth went back to college, selecting literature, poetry, short story writing, psychology, sociology, art history, and art.

Ruth was staff writer for *Kaleidoscope*, the publication of the Peninsula Poets Guild in Northern California, and poetry judge for *The Write*

Place. She taught creative writing, and established a poetry group for psychiatric patients at Marin General Hospital, merging with the art director's class. Amazing changes came about as patients, some who had never written before, expressed their deepest feelings and discovered their own hidden joy.

Ruth's first two books of poetry are titled, *Days of Together* and *Maybe Shirts Are Easier: A Path Back to Life*.

2009
Blessings And Curses, by New York poet Anne Whitehouse *(poetry)*

Anne Whitehouse was born and grew up in Birmingham, Alabama. She graduated from Harvard College and Columbia University. She is the author of *The Surveyor's Hand* (poems) and *Fall Love* (novel). Her second novel, *Rosalind's Ring,* set in Birmingham, is a finalist in the Santa Fe Writers Project Literary Awards. Her poetry chapbook, *Bear in Mind,* is forthcoming from Finishing Line Press. She lives in New York City with her husband and daughter. (www.annewhitehouse.com)

Dingle Day, by Irish poet Joe O'Connell *(poetry)*

Joe O'Connell holds a Ph.D. in biochemistry and is a Senior Lecturer in the Department of Medicine at University College Cork, Ireland. Editor of RT-PCR Protocols (2002), he has contributed numerous articles and reviews to scientific journals. O'Connell's work includes the seminal discovery of what he termed the "FasCounteratttack" — a mechanism by which cancers elude the immune system. O'Connell was awarded a Centennial Prize for Academic Publishing in Medical and Health Sciences by the National University of Ireland in 2009. A native of Portmagee, County Kerry, O'Connell resides with his wife and son in Cork City. *Dingle Day* is his first published collection of poetry.

Render, by Joseph Zaccardi *(poetry)*

Nominated for a Northern California Book Award. Poet Laureate of Marin County, CA 2013-2015.

Joseph Zaccardi served as Marin County, CA poet laureate (2013-2015), and during his tenure published and edited *Changing Harm to Harmony: Bullies & Bystanders Project*. His poems have been published in *Cincinnati Review, Common Ground Review, Poet Lore, Spillway*, and elsewhere;

his fourth collection of poems, *A Wolf Stands Alone in Water,* was published by *CW Books* 2015.

THE GATHERING, BY DIANA FESTA *(POETRY)*

Diana Festa grew up in Italy and came to the United States at the age of eighteen. She studied at American Universities. After earning a doctorate, she began her academic career as professor of French at Brooklyn College and the Graduate Center of The City University of New York. She was also a psychotherapist with a private practice. Diana Festa published a large number of articles and four books on literary criticism, Les Nouvelles de Balzac, The City as Catalyst, Balzac, Proustian Optics. As a poet, she published four volumes of poetry, Arches to the West, Ice Sparrow, Thresholds, Bedrock, and numerous poems in various reviews. Her honors include the Prix Guizot from the French Academy, a Guggenheim Fellowship, The Aniello Lauri Award, and several poetry prizes. She passed on June 8, 2011 at 80 years old.

THE BELLS OF AVALON, SHAMANIC POETRY OF BRIAN BRONSON, PM BOOKS *(POETRY)*

Brian Bronson has been writing poetry since he was a teenager. He studied English and History at the University of California, Irvine and then moved on to do a joint degree in law and public administration at Syracuse University with a concentration in Children's Welfare. Brian works as a law clerk for his father, a criminal appellate practitioner, representing indigent clients in Los Angeles. Brian is also moving into mediation, and has been admitted to the LA Superior Court Mediation Panel.

AND SO IT IS: ESSAYS ON THE SPIRITUAL LIFE, BY REVEREND JAMES FOX, PM LIBRARY *(NON-FICTION)*

Jim Fox grew up on a farm in West Virginia. He attended church with his family, took part in church activities and studied the Bible in group classes at Sunday School. He graduated from High School in 1952 in time to be drafted into the military during the Korean Conflict. After two years serving his country Jim worked as a mechanic for twenty-five years in Ohio before moving to California in 1979.

He and his wife Joanna found the Science of Mind teaching in 1986 and attended all the classes the Science of Mind had to offer and, after five years of studies, they became ministers. In 1994 they founded the Spiritual Awareness Center located in Madera, California.

2008
Finding Passage, by Molly Weller, PM Books *(poetry)*

Molly Weller is an author, teacher, career counselor, and quilter. In a previous life, she was a chef. Ms. Weller lives in Colorado, where she spends as much time as possible sitting under pine trees and investigating local bakeries with her husband John Thompson. She has previous publications in American, Canadian, and Israeli literary journals, as well as two published collections of poetry, the most recent of which was *Finding Passage* published by PM Books. In addition to writing, Ms. Weller works for Metropolitan State University of Denver as the Assistant Director of Work-Based Learning and teaches English at the community college level.

Untitled, by Richard Kovac PM Books *(poetry)*
for bio see *The Benign Tree*

2007
News of the Day: Poems of the Times, by John (Peterson) *(poetry)*
for bio see *the nature of mountains*

The Unequivocality of a Rose, by Joel Netsky *(poetry)*
Winner of the Poetic Matrix Press Slim Volume Poetry Prize.

Joel Netsky was born in Philadelphia. While at college he studied literature and writing, and in the years following developed a personal poetry writing style based upon a naturalistic rendering of poetic structures. "I then became 'religious': life metamorphosed to a spiritual journey. This is not to say that I attained any insights beyond the mundane, but life to me from then on became aspiration toward a supernal. I did very little writing during that time, worked more on myself internally, and only gradually did I return to writing."

Trial and Error: The Education of a Freedom Lawyer—Volume One: For the Defense, by Law Professor Arthur W. Campbell *(poetic prose)*
for bio see *Trial and Error Volume III*

2006
IN A DRESS MADE OF BUTTERFLIES, BY SANDRA LEE STILLWELL (POETRY)

Sandra Lee Stillwell is a wild flower transplanted in full bloom from the Mendocino Coast to the inlands of California. "I am a descendant of the Karuk People of Northern California. My Grandmothers ventured from their brown eyed suitors to settle with husbands with beautiful sea green and sky blue eyes, hence only my heart is truly native. I carry a small grudge aimed at my Grandmothers to this day."

"In this first book I have tried to tell the stories of my life and the lives of others with as much truth as possible. In some cases I have failed miserably. Everyday brings a new dawn and another chance to get it right, another chance to cherish all of life's blessings, another chance to dream of and work toward peace for all of the Earth's children."

OF ONE AND MANY WORLDS, BY BUDDHIST POET RAYN ROBERTS (POETRY)

Rayn Roberts is found in print and online at Chronogram, Rattle, Rattapallax, Retort Magazine, The Sow's Ear Review, Voices in Wartime, Opening of The Heart, PoetsWest, Thunder Sandwich, The Pedestal Magazine, Fireweed, Sauce Box, Gypsy Magazine, Tamafyhr Mountain Poetry, Turbula, Void Magazine, Poet's Corner in Fieralingue, Poetic Voices and others. He appears in four anthologies, "In the Arms of Words: Poems for Distaster Relief" from Sherman Asher & Foothill Publishing, "The Book of Hope" & "The World Healing Book" from Beyond Borders Press and "Paths" from The Philosophical Library of Escondido, California. These books include new and established poets Lawrence Ferlinghetti, Rita Dove, Marilyn Chin & a great voice for peace, The Dalai Lama. In 2006, Evolving Editions Press in New York included Rayn in their " Illuminations" series, volume three. "Illuminations" is concerned with interfaith understanding through poetry, art, photography and interviews. "Of One and Many Worlds" is his third book. In 2003 he toured the U.S. to promote, "Jazz Cocktails & Soapbox Songs". He is also the author of "The Fires of Spring", a collection of Buddhist poems written in South Korea. Website: www.geocities.com/raynrobkorea

NATURE JOURNAL WITH JOHN MUIR,
EDITED BY BONNIE JOHANNA GISEL *(WRITING JOURNAL)*
Bonnie Johanna Gisel is a naturalist, artist, nature writer, and historian who has written extensively about the life and work of John Muir. Presently she is at work on a book on John Muir and his life as a botanist. She is the author of the introduction to John Muir: Family, Friends, and Adventures and the author and editor of Kindred & Related Spirits: The Letters of John Muir and Jeanne C. Carr. She has published articles and lectured on John Muir and her own journeys in wilderness, including "A Song in Several Keys. Yosemite Journal," that appeared in California Tour and Travel. Bonnie is the curator at the Sierra Club's LeConte Memorial Lodge in Yosemite National Park, where she designs environmental education programs including the "Nature Journal," the Wilderness Quilt Project, Words for Wilderness Around the World, and Green Shoes.

THE LOST PILGRIMAGE POEMS, BY JOSEPH D. MILOSCH *(POETRY)*
for bio see *Landscape of a Woman and a Hummingbird*

2005
WINDS OF CHANGE / VIENTOS DE CAMBIO, BY TOMÁS GAYTON (BILINGUAL POETRY)
for bio see *Sojourn on the Bohemian Highway*

CHANGE (WILL DO YOU GOOD), BY GAIL ENTREKIN *(POETRY)*
Chosen for the Poetic Matrix Press Slim Volume Poetry Prize and nominated for a Northern California Book Award.
for bio see *The Art of Healing*

THE FM. LITERARY ANTHOLOGY / CELEBRATING 10 YEARS OF LITERARY HARASSMENT *(SPECIAL PROJECT)*
Madera High School students collection of poetry and art over 10 years, Madera California. Faculty Advisor: Darren Klasse; Editor: Devon Peterson

2004
MERGE WITH THE RIVER, BY YOSEMITE POET JAMES DOWNS *(POETRY)*
James Downs is a native Texan, James moved to the Golden State in 1993, and proudly considers himself a 'permanent Californian.' While

living and working in Yosemite National Park for 20 years, James produced a twice yearly onstage writer's night, WORDS, for 11 of those years. In the past, James produced a number of hand written poetry chapbooks and since has been published twice by POETIC MATRIX PRESS...a chapbook, WHERE MANZANITA in 2000 and a full volume, MERGE WITH THE RIVER in 2004 (he is working on his third volume, to be entitled THE SKIN OF ALL THINGS). Since 2010, James has also been Associate Editor for the PRESS and loves his duty of finding good new poets to publish.

James's happiest occasion was marrying his love Joy (who he met at Yosemite) under a giant willow tree along an ancient creek on his publisher's land in 2007. Together they just celebrated their tenth anniversary by sharing an evening out having wonderful Italian food. James retired and he and Joy now have a home in Sonora, California with two cats, Belle and Angel, and their adult daughter Samantha and her dog Lillie. Joy and Samantha work at Black Oak Casino in Tuolumne, California up the road. In their spare time, Joy and James are in the Community Chorus of Sonora and also the Congregational Church Choir of Murphys, CA. And both are students at Columbia College of Columbia, CA. And still they are happy to be Californians."

2003
DRIVEN INTO THE SHADE, BY BRANDON CESMAT *(POETRY)*
Winner of the 2003 San Diego Book Award for Poetry.
for bio see *Light in All Directions*

2002
Chapbook
> Letting in the Light by London poet Joan Michelson, 2002.

2001
DARK HILLS AND WILD MOUNTAINS, BY JOHN *(POETRY)*
for bio see the nature of mountains

Chapbooks
> Solstice by Kathryn Kruger, 2001.
> The Last Known Photograph of Daphne
> > by Anthony Russell White, 2001.

2000
Chapbooks
> Mountain Fireflies by Jeff Mann, 2000.
> ZERO by Grace Marie Grafton, 2000.
> uzumite - poems of Yosemite, by John Peterson, 2000.
> Where Manzanita by James Downs, 2000.

1997-2017
Newsletter

20th ANNIVERSARY AUTHORS' ANTHOLOGY

www.ingramcontent.com/pod-product-compliance
Lightning Source LLC
Chambersburg PA
CBHW030853170426
43193CB00009BA/592